NAUTICAL QUILTS

NAUTICAL QUILTS

*12 stitched and quilted
projects celebrating the sea*

Lynette Anderson

www.sewandso.co.uk

Dedication

In memory of Grandad Barnes, who sailed the Seven Seas and always had magical tales of far-off places to tell his grandchildren.

Contents

Introduction

The sights, sounds and smells of the ocean are a key part of every sailor's life. Whether you're in the Navy as my Grandad Barnes was, a professional sailor like my stepson Sean, or a weekend hobby sailor, the sea is in your blood. In this book I have created twelve projects that can be made to celebrate a nautical life or to add an ocean feel to our homes. The idea of the Nautical Flag Quilt has been in my mind for several years so it has been very exciting to see the final quilt completed. All the projects have been made using fabric from the ranges I've designed, and I took great pleasure from matching lots of different collections to get a gorgeous scrappy look. I hope that you will enjoy making a nautical quilt for someone you love and have lots of fun making the smaller projects that can be found within these pages.

MEASUREMENTS

Imperial and metric measurements have been given in the book, with metric in brackets (parenthesis). The projects were made using Imperial measurements, so the best results will be obtained using this system. Read all the project instructions before you start, to familarize yourself with what is required. The projects use a ¼in (6mm) seam allowance, unless otherwise stated.

FABRICS

At the start of each project there is a 'You Will Need' list that describes the fabrics needed and the quantity. Fabric quantities are based on a 42in (107cm) width of fabric, unless otherwise stated.

DIAGRAMS

Drawings have been given to illustrate the stepped text where necessary. These are not to scale but are just intended to support the text.

BASIC TECHNIQUES

All of the projects have the instructions, diagrams and photographs you need to make them successfully. There are a few techniques that are common to many of the projects and these are given in a section at the back of the book (see Techniques). It is a good idea to read through this section before you start any project.

Appliqué and embroidery are favourite techniques of mine, especially traditional needle-turn appliqué. The projects can use either needle-turn appliqué or fusible web appliqué. Both methods are described in detail in the Basic Techniques section. Just remember that needle-turn appliqué requires a small seam allowance around each motif, usually ⅛in–¼in (3mm–6mm). Fusible web appliqué does not need a seam allowance because the edges are normally oversewn in some way, usually with blanket stitch. If using the templates for fusible web appliqué you will need to reverse (flip) them before use.

TEMPLATES

One of my favourite parts of quilting is the appliqué and stitchery, so most of the projects use templates. These have been provided full size in the Templates section at the back of the book. Some of the templates need joining so read the instructions carefully.

Materials & Equipment

The projects each have a list of the materials and equipment required and the basics are described here, but there's no reason why you can't experiment, especially with fabrics and embellishments.

Fabrics & wadding (batting)

For many people, 100 per cent cotton fabrics are the ones of choice for patchwork and quilting but sometimes it's great to try other types of fabric. The fabrics used to back quilts, bind quilts or to line projects such as bags can really be anything you like but cotton is the easiest to handle.

Quilt wadding (batting) is rated by its weight and is sold in standard sizes and by the yard or metre. It is available in polyester, cotton, wool and various blends and for hand and machine quilting. Thinner wadding tends to be used when machine quilting. I prefer to use Matilda's Own wool/poly blend, which is pre-washed, pre-shrunk, fully machine washable and comes in white and charcoal.

Threads

Many people like to use 100 per cent cotton thread for machine piecing and machine quilting. Polyester mixes are also popular. Threads for hand quilting can be almost anything you like. If you want the quilting to blend or tone with the fabrics then use a cotton or polyester.

For my stitcheries I mostly use Valdani, Cosmo and occasionally DMC stranded cotton (floss). These embroidery threads are in six-stranded skeins that can be split into separate strands and are available in a wide range of colours. Valdani threads are hand-dyed which means they have subtle shading and variegation of colour throughout the skein. To get a good variation of colour when working on small areas of embroidery, I often cut two short, say 10in (25.4cm), lengths of Valdani cotton (floss) from colour A and B. I start the embroidery by working with two strands from A then work with two strands from B and keep alternating to get the desired effect.

DMC alternatives to Valdani have been provided here although please note that the colour matches aren't exact as DMC cotton (floss) is a solid colour.

Valdani code/colour	DMC code
#H204 nostalgic rose	#3858
#JP12 seaside	#927
#P4 aged white	#712
#P5 tarnished gold	#3852
#P10 antique violet	#3041
#031 tealish blue	#927
#078 aged wine	#221
#154 antique gold	#420
#512 chimney dust	#451
#514 wheat husk	#739
#518 dusty leaves	#3781
#539 evergreens	#319
#548 blackened khaki	#3031
#575 crispy leaf	#3364
#0126 old cottage grey	#413
#0178 tea	#3782
#0510 terracotta twist	#921
#0511 black sea	#310
#0578 primitive blue	#931

Fusible web & interfacing

Fusible web is also referred to as iron-on adhesive and is an ultra-thin sheet of adhesive backed with a special paper. When the web is placed between two fabrics, the heat of an iron causes the glue to melt and fuse the fabrics together -- perfect for appliqué (see Basic Techniques: Fusible Web Appliqué). There are various makes of fusible web, including Bondaweb (also called Vliesofix or Wonder Under) and Steam-A-Seam2. Read the manufacturer's instructions before use.

Fusible interfacing works on the same principle but is single-sided. It is used to stiffen and strengthen fabrics.

An iron-on stabilizer can also be used to strengthen a fabric, making it more able to support embroidery stitches. It needs to be ironed on before the stitching is started. I always cut mine approximately ¼in (6mm) smaller than the background fabric.

Buttons

I like to use buttons in my work, not just functional ones but also to represent animal eyes, flower centres and so on. I have my own range of really cute buttons in all sorts of shapes. Some are raw wood, while others have been hand painted in Australia – see Suppliers.

Equipment

There are many tools and gadgets you could buy for patchwork and quilting but a basic tool kit is all you really need to start with.

Basic tool kit			
☑	Quilter's ruler	☑	Template plastic
☑	Rotary cutter and mat	☑	Marking pen
☑	Scissors	☑	Iron
☑	Tape measure	☑	Sewing machine
☑	Needles	☑	Embroidery hoop
☑	Pins and safety pins	☑	Fabric glue
☑	Thimble	☑	Suitable threads

Cutting tools

Patchwork is easier and quicker with a rotary cutter, mat and quilter's ruler, especially for quilt making. You will find an 18in x 24in self-healing cutting mat is very useful and a 45mm or 60mm diameter rotary cutter.

Pins & needles

You will need pins for piecing patchwork and for fastening the layers of a quilt together. Safety pins could also be used for securing the quilt sandwich. Alternatively, spray adhesives are available for this.

You will need a selection of hand sewing needles for embroidery and quilting, and machine needles for piecing and quilting. For hand sewing I like to use a milliner's needle. The long eye is easy to thread, and it is fine enough to glide through the fabric.

Marking pens

In this book markers are mostly used to mark stitchery designs onto fabric. I use a fine Zig Millenium or Pigma Micron permanent marker pen, usually in brown. There are also water- and air-soluble pens that can be used to mark fabric temporarily.

Template plastic

This is a transparent plastic that can be used to create templates, which can be used many times. It is available from craft shops and patchwork and quilting suppliers. The template is traced onto the plastic and cut out with sharp scissors (don't use your fabric scissors!). Use a permanent marker to label the template.

Masking tape

This is useful to mark straight quilting lines. Simply place a long strip of the tape where you want to quilt and sew along the edge of the tape. A low-tack tape is easy to remove and doesn't leave any marks.

Appliqué mat

An appliqué mat is a large non-stick sheet, usually made from Teflon. One advantage to using an appliqué mat is that you can iron some of the underneath pieces in place, thus stopping them moving out of position, which allows you to place the top layers with ease. You can remove and re-position fabrics fused to an appliqué mat, but not fabrics already fused to fabrics. Keep your mat rolled up when not in use and it will last for years.

Apliquick™ tools

The revolutionary Apliquick™ tools were developed by my friend Rosa Rojas. The two rods are made from steel, which give them a nice feel in your hands as you work with them. The thicker of the rods has a forked end and this is the rod that you hold the appliqué pieces in place with. The other rod has a bevelled edge for turning and pressing the seam allowance to the wrong side of the fabric. Both rods have a fine point on the other end, which is used when working with very small pieces.

Tip

If patchwork and embroidery is a new craft for you then taking a class is a great way to get started and to learn good habits. Classes can be found at your local quilt store or search the internet as many classes are now available online.

Appliqué paper

This comes in sheet form and is a single-sided, fusible water-soluble paper, making it ideal for use with the Apliquick™ tools or as a replacement for the traditional pre-cut papers for English paper piecing. The paper can be put through an inkjet printer, which enables you to print multiple pieces of the same shape without the need to laboriously draw them by hand. The paper does not need to be removed from the completed work, as it softens with handling and disintegrates when the finished project is washed.

Black grip mat

This mat, the modern equivalent of a sandpaper board, is ideal for preventing fabrics from moving as you trace appliqué shapes and when you are working with the Apliquick™ tools. It is light and can be stored by rolling up when not in use. It can be hand washed to remove any unwanted glue residue that's left from working English paper piecing or the Apliquick™ method of preparing your shapes for appliqué.

Glues

There are temporary glues available that are very useful, especially for appliqué. I find Roxanne's Glue Baste-It™ excellent as it has a fine nozzle for accurate placement of the glue. It is only a temporary glue but is handy for holding pieces in place instead of using pins. A fabric glue pen is used in the preparation of English paper pieces and in the preparation of appliqué shapes when using the Apliquick™ tools. You will also need a clear drying craft glue for fixing the Ship Ahoy Snip Cover together. Always follow the instructions on the packet and use in a well-ventilated room.

Light box or light pad

A light box is a useful piece of equipment for tracing designs but can be expensive so try a light pad, or for no cost at all use a well-lit window. Tape the design to the light box (or pad or window), tape the fabric on top and trace the design onto the fabric. I also use a light under a glass table, which works well and stops my arms getting tired when standing at a window!

Projects

Nautical Flag Quilt

This bold quilt is inspired by nautical flags, a unique way that seafarers can send messages to other boats or back to shore and which can be used singularly or in combination with other flags. There is a different flag for each letter of the alphabet and each letter also has a specific meaning such as 'diver down' or 'keep clear'. Here, I have included block patterns for all the letters of the nautical alphabet, but you could have fun making the relevant letter blocks to spell out a name or word. I decided to make my quilt with a coordinated scrappy feel and had lots of fun selecting the fabrics from my stash.

You will need...

⚓ Selection of fabric for the blocks (see individual block instructions)

⚓ Light beige tonal fabric for the sashing and borders 2⅝yd (2.5m)

⚓ Selection of prints for the pieced border, a total of 1⅛yd (1.1m)

⚓ Grey fabric for the outer border 1¼yd (1.2m)

⚓ Wadding (batting) 100in (254cm) square

⚓ Backing fabric 100in (254cm) square

⚓ Dark green fabric for the binding ⅞yd (0.8m)

Finished size

94in (239cm) square approx.

Each block is 12in (30.5cm) square

Use ¼in (6mm) seams unless otherwise stated

A TO Z OF NAUTICAL FLAGS

When used singularly these square flags send an important message back to the shore or to other ships at sea. Their meaning can also vary, for example when used at a regatta or if flown in combination with other flags. Here are some of the standard one-flag signals:

A	Diver down
B	Dangerous goods
C	Yes or affirmative
D	Manoeuvring with difficulty; keep clear
E	Altering my course to starboard
F	I am disabled; communicate with me
G	I require a pilot
H	Pilot on board
I	I am altering my course to port
J	I am on fire and have dangerous cargo; keep clear
K	I wish to communicate with you
L	You should stop your vessel immediately
M	My vessel is stopped and making no way through the water
N	No or negative
O	Man overboard
P	All personnel return to ship; the vessel is about to proceed to sea (when used in port)
Q	Ship meets health regulations; request clearance into port
R	Preparing to replenish (when used at sea)
S	Moving astern
T	Keep clear; engaged in trawling
U	You are running into danger
V	I require assistance
W	I require medical assistance
X	Stop carrying out your intentions and watch for my signals
Y	I am dragging anchor
Z	I require a tug

CUTTING AND CONSTRUCTION FOR ALPHABET BLOCKS

Making Letter A

1. From Fabric A1 cut:
   - One 6½in x 12½in (16.5cm x 31.8cm) rectangle.
   - One A shape using the template provided.

2. From Fabric A2 cut:
   - One 1½in x 12½in (3.8cm x 31.8cm) strip.
   - One B shape using the template provided.
   - One C shape using the template provided.

3. Sew the Fabric A2 B and C shapes to opposite sides of the Fabric A1 A shape to create a rectangle (**Fig 1a**).

4. Arrange and sew the Fabric A2 strip to the left of the sewn unit, followed by the Fabric A1 rectangle (**Fig 1b**).

Fig 1a

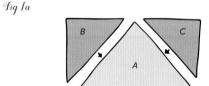

Fig 1b

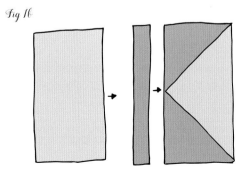

Making Letter B

1. From Fabric B1 cut:

   - One 6½in x 12½in (16.5cm x 31.8cm) rectangle.

   - Two 6½in (16.5cm) squares.

2. From Fabric B2 cut one 6½in x 12½in (16.5cm x 31.8cm) rectangle.

3. Draw a diagonal line on the wrong side of one Fabric B1 square. Place the square, right sides together, at a corner of the Fabric B2 rectangle. Sew on the drawn line. Trim ¼in (6mm) away from the line and press open. Repeat with the other Fabric B1 square on the opposite side to complete the flying geese unit (**Fig 2a to 2c**).

4. Sew the Fabric B1 rectangle to the left of the flying geese unit (**Fig 2d**).

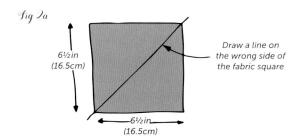

Fig 2a

6½in (16.5cm)

6½in (16.5cm)

Draw a line on the wrong side of the fabric square

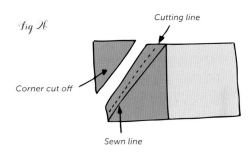

Fig 2b

Cutting line

Corner cut off

Sewn line

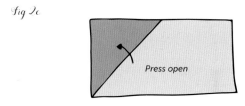

Fig 2c

Press open

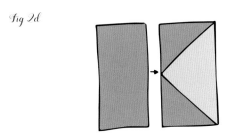

Fig 2d

Making Letter C

1. From Fabric C1 cut one 12½in x 3in (31.8cm x 7.6cm) rectangle.

2. From Fabric C2 cut two 12½in x 2⅞in (31.8cm x 7.3cm) rectangles.

3. From Fabric C3 cut two 12½in x 2⅞in (31.8cm x 7.3cm) rectangles.

4. Arrange and sew together a Fabric C2 rectangle to the top and bottom of the Fabric C1 rectangle, followed by a Fabric C3 rectangle.

Making Letter D

1. From Fabric D1 cut two 12½in x 4½in (31.8cm x 11.4cm) rectangles.

2. From Fabric D2 cut one 12½in x 4½in (31.8cm x 11.4cm) rectangle.

3. Arrange and sew together a Fabric D1 rectangle to each side of the Fabric D2 rectangle.

Making Letter E

1. From Fabric E1 cut one 12½in x 6½in (31.8cm x 16.5cm) rectangle.

2. From Fabric E2 cut one 12½in x 6½in (31.8cm x 16.5cm) rectangle.

3. Arrange and sew together a Fabric E2 rectangle to the bottom of the Fabric E1 rectangle.

Making Letter F

1. From Fabric F1 cut four 6½in (16.5cm) squares.

2. From Fabric F2 cut one 12½in (31.8cm) square.

3. Draw a diagonal line on the wrong side of one 6½in (16.5cm) Fabric F1 square. Place the square, right sides together, at a corner of the Fabric F2 square. Sew on drawn line. Trim ¼in (6mm) away from the line and press open (Fig 3a and 3b).

4. Repeat with the other three Fabric F1 squares, sewing one to each corner.

Fig 3a

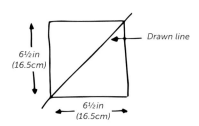

6½in (16.5cm)

6½in (16.5cm)

Drawn line

Fig 3b

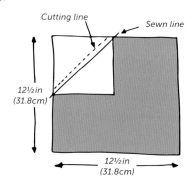

Cutting line

Sewn line

12½in (31.8cm)

12½in (31.8cm)

Making Letter G

1. From Fabric G1 cut three 2½in x 12½in (6.4cm x 31.8cm) rectangles.

2. From Fabric G2 cut three 2½in x 12½in (6.4cm x 31.8cm) rectangles.

3. Arrange and sew together, alternating the Fabric G1 and G2 rectangles.

Making Letter J

1. From Fabric J1 cut two 4in x 12½in (10.2cm x 31.8cm) rectangles.

2. From Fabric J2 cut one 5½in x 12½in (14cm x 31.8cm) rectangle.

3. Arrange and sew a Fabric J1 rectangle to the top and bottom of the Fabric J2 rectangle.

Making Letter H

1. From Fabric H1 cut one 6½in x 12½in (16.5cm x 31.8cm) rectangle.

2. From Fabric H2 cut one 6½in x 12½in (16.5cm x 31.8cm) rectangle.

3. Arrange and sew together a Fabric H2 rectangle to the right-hand side of the fabric H1 rectangle.

Making Letter K

1. From Fabric K1 cut one 6½in x 12½in (16.5cm x 31.8cm) rectangle.

2. From Fabric K2 cut one 6½in x 12½in (16.5cm x 31.8cm) rectangle.

3. Arrange and sew together the Fabric K2 rectangle to the right-hand side of the fabric K1 rectangle.

Making Letter I

1. From Fabric I1 cut one 12½in (31.8cm) square.

2. Using your favourite method of appliqué, take Fabric I2 and prepare a circle using the template provided. I used the needle-turn method (see Basic Techniques: Appliqué).

3. Position the circle in the centre of the Fabric I1 square. Once you are happy with the placement, appliqué the circle in place.

Making Letter L

1. From Fabric L1 cut two 6½in (16.5cm) squares.

2. From Fabric L2 cut two 6½in (16.5cm) squares.

3. Arrange the squares in a four-by-four arrangement. Sew together to make two rows, then sew the rows together.

Making Letter M

1. From Fabric M1 cut:
   - Two A shapes using the template provided.
   - One B shape using the template provided.

2. From Fabric M2 cut four C shapes using the template provided.

3. Sew a Fabric M2 C shape to the opposite long sides of a Fabric M1 A shape. Repeat to make a second unit.

4. Sew the units to the opposite long sides of the Fabric M1 B shape.

Making Letter O

1. From Fabric O1 cut one 13in (33cm) square.

2. From Fabric O2 cut one 13in (33cm) square.

3. Draw a diagonal line on the wrong side of the Fabric O1 square using a suitable fabric marker (I prefer a 2B pencil). Place the square on top of the Fabric O2 square, right sides together. Sew ¼in (6mm) away from, and on both sides of, the drawn line.

4. Cut along the drawn line. Open and press to yield two half-square triangle units. You will only use one in this quilt so put one aside (or you can use it for your quilt label). Align the diagonal seam of the half-square triangle unit to the 45-degree line on your quilting ruler and trim the unit to measure 12½in (31.8cm) square.

Making Letter N

1. From Fabric N1 cut eight 3½in (8.9cm) squares.

2. From Fabric N2 cut eight 3½in (8.9cm) squares.

3. Arrange and sew the sixteen squares into rows as follows:
   - Row 1 and 3 – Fabric N1, Fabric N2, Fabric N1, Fabric N2
   - Row 2 and 4 – Fabric N2, Fabric N1, Fabric N2, Fabric N1

4. Sew the rows together.

Making Letter P

1. From Fabric P1 cut one 6½in (16.5cm) square.

2. From Fabric P2 cut:
   - Two 3½in x 6½in (8.9cm x 16.5cm) rectangles.
   - Two 12½in x 3½in (31.8cm x 8.9cm) rectangles.

3. Sew the two 3½in x 6½in (8.9cm x 16.5cm) Fabric P2 rectangles to opposite sides of the Fabric P1 square.

4. Sew the two 12½in x 3½in (31.8cm x 8.9cm) Fabric P2 rectangles to the top and bottom of the unit.

Making Letter Q

1. From Fabric Q cut one 12½in (31.8cm) square.

Making Letter R

1. From Fabric R1 cut four 5½in (14cm) squares.

2. From Fabric R2 cut:
   - Two 2½in x 5½in (6.4cm x 14cm) rectangles.
   - One 12½in x 2½in (31.8cm x 6.4cm) rectangle.

3. Sew two 5½in (14cm) Fabric R1 squares to the opposite long sides of a 2½in x 5½in (6.4cm x 14cm) Fabric R2 rectangle to make a row. Repeat to make a second row.

4. Sew the rows to the top and bottom of the 12½in x 2½in (31.8cm x 6.4cm) Fabric R2 rectangle.

Making Letter S

1. From Fabric S1 cut one 6½in (16.5cm) square.

2. From Fabric S2 cut:
   - Two 3½in x 6½in (8.9cm x 16.5cm) rectangles.
   - Two 12½in x 3½in (31.8cm x 8.9cm) rectangles.

3. Sew the block, following the instructions for the Letter P block.

Making Letter T

1. From Fabric T1 cut one 4½in x 12½in (11.4cm x 31.8cm) rectangle.

2. From Fabric T2 cut one 4½in x 12½in (11.4cm x 31.8cm) rectangle.

3. From Fabric T3 cut one 4½in x 12½in (11.4cm x 31.8cm) rectangle.

4. Arrange and sew together the Fabric T2 and T3 rectangles to the opposite sides of the Fabric T1 rectangle.

Making Letter U

1. From Fabric U1 cut two 6½in (16.5cm) squares.

2. From Fabric U2 cut two 6½in (16.5cm) squares.

3. Sew the block, following the instructions for the Letter L block.

Making Letter V

1. From Fabric V1 cut:
   - Two A shapes using the template provided.
   - One B shape using the template provided.

2. From Fabric V2, cut four C shapes using the template provided.

3. Sew the block, following the instructions for the Letter M block.

Making Letter W

1. From Fabric W1 cut one 4½in (11.4cm) square.

2. From Fabric W2 cut:
   - Two 2½in x 4½in (6.4cm x 11.4cm) rectangles.
   - Two 8½in x 2½in (21.6cm x 6.4cm) rectangles.

3. From Fabric W3 cut:
   - Two 2½in x 8½in (6.4cm x 21.6cm) rectangles.
   - Two 12½in x 2½in (31.8cm x 6.4cm) rectangles.

4. Sew the two 2½in x 4½in (6.4cm x 11.4cm) Fabric W2 rectangles to opposite sides of the Fabric W1 square.

5. Sew the two 8½in x 2½in (21.6cm x 6.4cm) Fabric W2 rectangles to the top and bottom of the unit.

6. Sew the two 2½in x 8½in (6.4cm x 21.6cm) Fabric W3 rectangles to opposite sides of the unit, followed by the two 12½in x 2½in (31.8cm x 6.4cm) Fabric W3 rectangles to the top and bottom.

Making Letter X

1. From Fabric X1 cut four 5½in (14cm) squares.

2. From Fabric X2 cut:
   - Two 2½in x 5½in (6.4cm x 14cm) rectangles.
   - One 12½in x 2½in (31.8cm x 6.4cm) rectangle.

3. Sew the block, following the instructions for the Letter R block.

Making Letter Y/Z

MAKING THE Y UNIT (TOP LEFT)

1. From Fabric Y1 cut the following:
   - One A shape using the template provided.
   - Two C shapes using the template provided.
   - One E shape using the template provided.
   - One F shape using the template provided.

2. From Fabric Y2, cut the following:
   - Two B shapes using the template provided.
   - Two D shapes using the template provided.
   - One G shape using the template provided.

3. Arrange and sew the fabrics together to complete the Letter Y unit (Fig 4).

Fig 4

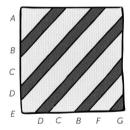

MAKING THE Z UNIT (BOTTOM RIGHT)

4 From Fabric Z1 cut one shape using the template provided.

5 From Fabric Z2 cut one shape using the template provided.

6 From Fabric Z3 cut one shape using the template provided.

7 From Fabric Z4 cut one shape using the template provided.

8 Lay out the triangles to form a square. Sew them together in pairs, then sew the pairs together (**Fig 5a and 5b**).

ASSEMBLING THE BLOCK

9 From Fabric YZ1 cut two 6½in (16.5cm) squares.

10 Arrange and sew together the Y and Z units and the two squares in a design two across and two down (**Fig 6**).

CUTTING OUT THE BORDERS

1 From the light beige tonal fabric cut the following:

- Seven strips 2½in (6.4cm) x width of fabric. Sub-cut the strips into twenty 2½in x 12½in (6.4cm x 31.8cm) strips for the sashing.

- Seven strips 2½in (6.4cm) x width of fabric. Join the strips and sub-cut into four 2½in x 68½in (6.4cm x 174cm) strips for the sashing.

- Seven strips 4in (10.2cm) x width of fabric. Join the strips and sub-cut into two 4in x 68½in (10.2cm x 174cm) strips and two 4in x 75½in (10.2cm x 191.8cm) strips for Border 1.

- Nine strips 3in (7.6cm) x width of fabric. Join the strips and sub-cut into two 3in x 81½in (7.6cm x 207cm) strips and two 3in x 86½in (7.6cm x 219.7cm) strips for Border 3.

2 From the selection of prints cut a total of 104 3½in (8.9cm) squares for Border 2.

3 From the grey fabric cut nine 4½in (11.4cm) x width of fabric strips. Join the strips and sub-cut into two 4½in x 86½in (11.4cm x 219.7cm) strips and two 4½in x 94½in (11.4cm x 240cm) strips for Border 4.

Fig 5a

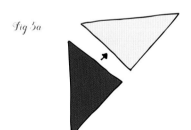

Fig 5b

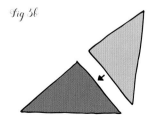
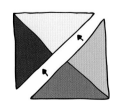

Fig 6

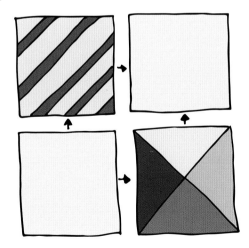

ASSEMBLING THE QUILT

1. Lay out the blocks into five rows, each with five blocks, placing a 2½in x 12½in (6.4cm x 31.8cm) light beige tonal strip between each block. Make sure your blocks are in alphabetical order and facing the same way as shown in **Fig 7**. Sew each row together.

2. Sew the rows together, placing a 2½in x 68½in (6.4cm x 174cm) light beige tonal strip between each one (**Fig 8**).

ADDING THE BORDERS

1. Sew the two 4in x 68½in (10.2cm x 174cm) light beige tonal strips to the sides of the quilt. Sew the two 4in x 75½in (10.2cm x 191.8cm) light beige tonal strips to the top and bottom of the quilt.

2. Arrange and sew together twenty-five assorted 3½in (8.9cm) squares to make a pieced row. Repeat to make a second row. Sew to the sides of the quilt.

3. Arrange and sew together twenty-seven assorted 3½in (8.9cm) squares to make a pieced row. Repeat to make a second row. Sew to the top and bottom of the quilt.

4. Sew the two 3in x 81½in (7.6cm x 207cm) light beige tonal strips to the sides of the quilt. Sew the two 3in x 86½in (7.6cm x 219.7cm) light beige tonal strips to the top and bottom of the quilt.

5. Sew two 4½in x 86½in (11.4cm x 219.7cm) grey strips to the sides of the quilt. Sew two 4½in x 94½in (11.4cm x 240cm) grey strips to the top and bottom of the quilt. This completes the quilt top.

Fig 7

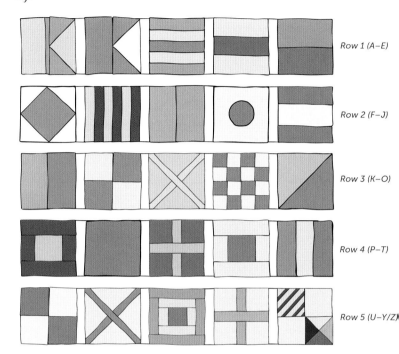

Row 1 (A–E)

Row 2 (F–J)

Row 3 (K–O)

Row 4 (P–T)

Row 5 (U–Y/Z)

Fig 8

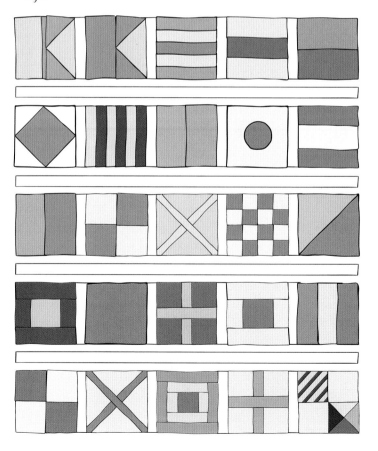

QUILTING AND FINISHING

1 Lay the pressed backing right side down on a surface, with the smoothed wadding (batting) on top. Lay the quilt top right side up on top, making sure there is wadding and backing showing all around, and then secure the layers together (see Basic Techniques: Making a Quilt Sandwich).

2 Quilt as desired. My quilt was custom quilted with an all over design called Plaid, designed by Patricia E. Ritter.

3 When all the quilting is finished, tidy up the thread ends, square up the quilt and prepare the binding. Cut ten strips of binding fabric, each 2½in (6.4cm) x width of fabric. Join the strips together using 45-degree seams. Press the seams open. Fold the strip in half all along the length, wrong sides together, and press. Use this strip to bind your quilt (see Basic Techniques: Binding). Add a label to your quilt recording your name and the date it was sewn.

Storm at Sea Picture

I have promised my husband a Storm at Sea quilt for as many years as I have known him but to date have still not made it, so this beautiful English paper pieced block with its sweet stitched border is my gift to him. There are sixty-five tiny pieces in the block which is just 4in (10.2cm) square when finished. It was sewn using the English paper piecing method and the small patches can make this block a little bit fiddly to make, but I hope you agree the end result is worth it. My frame was custom made using recycled fencing, but a shop-bought frame with the glass removed would work just as well.

You will need...

- ⚓ Cream tonal fabric for the embroidery background 10in (25.4cm) square
- ⚓ Assorted fabrics for the pieced block, each one a minimum size of 2½in (6.4cm) square
- ⚓ Pack of pre-cut paper templates for a 4in (10.2cm) Storm at Sea block (finished size)
- ⚓ Fabric glue pen (optional)
- ⚓ Fusible stitchery stabilizer (optional)

- ⚓ Valdani stranded embroidery cotton (floss): #0511 black sea, #0126 old cottage grey, #0178 tea, #JP12 seaside, #P5 tarnished gold, #078 aged wine, #548 blackened khaki, #0578 primitive blue
- ⚓ Fine-tipped fabric marking pen (removable if you prefer)
- ⚓ Frame to suit: I used one with an inside measurement of approx. 7in (17.8cm) square

Finished size

6½in (16.5cm) square approx. (unframed)

MAKING THE BLOCK

1. Following the main image, select your fabrics and decide where each one is going to be placed.

2. Prepare the shapes using an English paper piecing technique (see Basic Techniques: English Paper Piecing). Cut the fabric pieces approximately ¼in (6mm) larger than the templates. Centre a template on the wrong side of the fabric, wrap the fabric around the template, and either tack (baste) in place or use a glue pen (Fig 1).

3. Using a whip stitch, join the pieces together to make one centre and four corner units (Fig 2a and 2b), and four side units (Fig 2c).

4. Sew the units together to make three rows, then sew the rows together (Fig 3). Press the work firmly and remove the paper templates.

Tip

It is essential to buy pre-cut paper templates as they will ensure the tiny pieces fit together accurately. Cut your fabric ¼in (6mm) larger than the paper. Although it's tempting to cut the seam allowance smaller it is actually easier if it is ¼in (6mm). Use a fine thread and needle to stitch the pieces together, and remove the templates once the block is joined.

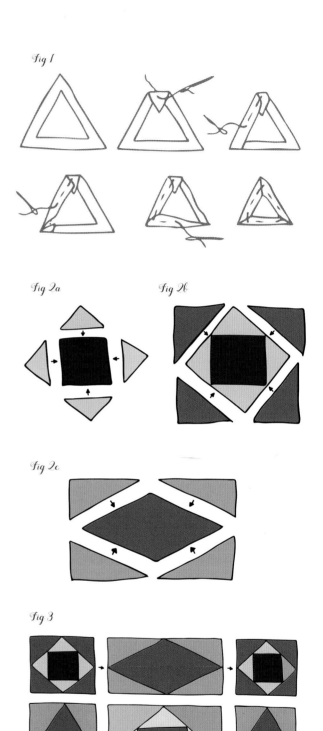

Fig 1

Fig 2a

Fig 2b

Fig 2c

Fig 3

TRANSFERRING THE STITCHERY DESIGN

5 Copy the stitchery pattern (see Templates). Using a light source such as a light box or a window, centre the cream tonal fabric right side up over the pattern. Using a fine-tipped fabric marking pen, carefully trace the stitchery lines.

6 If you are using an iron-on stitchery stabilizer – this will avoid thread shadows showing on the front of your work – fuse it to the back of the fabric before starting the embroidery. Place the shiny side of the stabilizer onto the wrong side of your fabric and bond it in place with an iron, following the manufacturer's instructions.

WORKING THE STITCHERY

7 Use two strands of Valdani embroidery thread to stitch the design. See Techniques: Embroidery Stitches for how to work the stitches and Materials & Equipment: Threads for DMC alternatives. Stitches used are (abbreviations in brackets): backstitch (BS), satin stitch (SS), running stitch (RS) and French knots (FN). When all embroidery is completed press the work carefully.

MAKING UP

8 Position the block in the centre of the stitchery and, using a blind hem stitch, appliqué the block in place.

9 Frame your work, then display and enjoy.

Key for threads and stitches

 #0511 Black sea

Little fish eyes, single strand (FN)

Anchor on large sailing boat (BS)

Hull of container ship (BS)

Portholes on container ship (fill with BS)

 #0126 Old cottage grey

Whale (BS)

Tail markings on whale (RS)

Whale eye (FN)

Whale mouth (BS)

Seagulls (BS with FN for bodies)

 #0178 Tea

Rock that the lighthouse sits on (BS)

Sails on tiny sailing boat (BS)

Container ship funnels and smoke (BS)

 #JP12 Seaside

Whale water spout (BS)

Sails on large sailing boat (BS)

Small fish (BS)

 #P5 Tarnished gold

Outline of beacon on the lighthouse (BS)

Light rays from beacon (BS)

Starfish (BS)

Back container on container boat (BS)

 #078 Aged wine

Lighthouse neck (fill with BS)

Flags on all sailing boats (SS)

Front container on container boat (BS)

Waterline on container boat (fill with BS)

Lines on container ship funnels (fill with BS)

#548 Blackened khaki

Astragal bars on beacon (BS)

Window on lighthouse (SS)

Hull of large sailing boat (BS and RS)

Dashed lines on large sailing boat (BS)

Hull of small sailing boat (fill with BS)

Masts of small and large sailing boats (BS)

Lighthouse door (BS with a FN doorknob)

 #0578 Primitive blue

Line of the ocean (BS)

Lighthouse tower (BS)

Waves in the ocean (BS)

Ship Ahoy Needleroll and Snip Cover

This set is inspired by days gone by when every sailor had a basic sewing roll for the simple repairs that needed doing when on a long voyage. I wanted my roll to not only be practical but also reflect the sea, so started by sewing tiny clamshells together to make a delightfully scaly looking cover. Handy storage was then added inside, a sweet embroidered scene sewn to the front, and it was finished off with a coordinating snip cover. For ease, my clamshells were sewn using pre-cut semi-soluble paper liners that do not have to be removed after sewing.

Ship Ahoy Needleroll

You will need...

- Light grey tonal fabric for the embroidery background 10in (25.4cm) square
- Assorted blue printed fabric, about 150 pieces each 1¾in (4.4cm) square
- Contrast blue print for the inner pocket 5in (12.7cm) square
- Blue tonal fabric for the lining and button loop 12in x 8in (30.5cm x 20.3cm)
- Blue/mauve print for the needleroll ends 8in (20.3cm) square
- Three pieces of wool for the fish needle keepers, each approx. 3in x 4in (7.6cm x 10.2cm)
- Scraps of blue wool for the fish fins
- Muddy green wool for the front 3in x 5in (7.6cm x 12.7cm)
- Valdani stranded embroidery cotton (floss): #548 blackened khaki, #0578 primitive blue, #H204 nostalgic rose, #154 antique gold, #JP12 seaside, #0511 black sea, #512 chimney dust
- Approx. 150 pre-cut clamshell templates each 1in (2.5cm), I used the semi-soluble leave-in variety
- Fusible web
- Lightweight fusible wadding (batting) 12in x 8in (30.5cm x 20.3cm)
- Fine-tipped fabric marking pen (removable if you prefer)
- Two 1¼in (3.2cm) diameter plastic domes (see Suppliers)
- One ¾in (1.9cm) diameter vintage mother of pearl button
- Thin card 4½in (11.4cm) square
- Craft glue

Finished size

5in x 9½in (12.7cm x 24.1cm) approx. (when open)

Use ¼in (6mm) seams unless otherwise stated

TRANSFERRING THE STITCHERY DESIGNS

1 Copy the stitchery patterns (see Templates). Using a light source such as a light box or window, centre the light grey tonal fabric right side up over the pattern. Use a fabric pen to carefully trace the stitchery designs. You need one boat oval and two bird circles.

WORKING THE STITCHERY

2 Use two strands of embroidery thread to stitch the design. See Techniques: Embroidery Stitches for how to work the stitches and Materials & Equipment: Threads for DMC alternatives. Stitches used are (abbreviations in brackets): backstitch (BS), satin stitch (SS), chain stitch (CHS) and French knots (FN). When stitching is completed, press gently and cut on the outer lines (shown in blue on the templates).

Key for threads and stitches

 #548 Blackened khaki
Sailing boat (BS)
Outer line (BS)

 #0578 Primitive blue
Ocean (CHS)

 #H204 Nostalgic rose
Flag on sailing boat (SS)
Front little fish in the sea (BS)
Seagulls (BS)

 #154 Antique gold
Seagull beaks (BS)

 #JP12 Seaside
Little fish in the sea (BS)
Seagull wings (SS)

 #0511 Black sea
Seagull legs (BS)
Seagull eyes (FN)
Gulls in sky (BS with FN bodies)
Fish eyes (FN)

 #512 Chimney dust
Sails (BS)

MAKING THE CLAMSHELL PANEL

3 Centre a paper clamshell on the wrong side of a piece of blue printed fabric and either glue in place or use a pin. Cut the fabric ¼in (6mm) away from the paper. Next, fold the excess fabric over the paper and tack (baste) in place or use a glue pen (**Fig 1a and 1b**). I used semi-soluble paper clamshells which do not have to be removed after sewing. Prepare approximately 145 clamshells from the assorted blue prints.

4 Lay out twenty-six rows of clamshells, alternating between six and five in a row. Join them together into rows by taking a couple of tiny stitches at the point where each of the clamshells meet (**Fig 2a**). Once the rows have been joined appliqué each row on top of the previous one using a blind hem stitch, making sure the tiny joining stitches are covered (**Fig 2b**). The panel needs to measure at least 5in x 11½in (12.7cm x 29.2cm).

Fig 1a

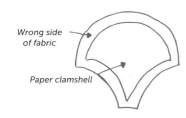

Wrong side of fabric

Paper clamshell

Fig 1b

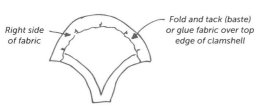

Right side of fabric

Fold and tack (baste) or glue fabric over top edge of clamshell

Fig 2a

Stitch here to hold clamshells together

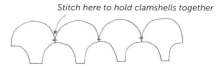

Fig 2b

Appliqué each row on top of the previous one

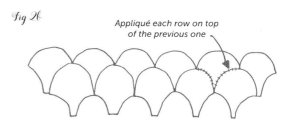

5 Give the clamshells a press and trim the panel to 5in x 11½in (12.7cm x 29.2cm).

Tip

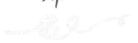

If you decide to hand cut paper clamshells from the template provided in the Templates section then it is essential to be accurate when cutting or you risk the clamshells not fitting together properly. These papers cannot be left in, so need to be removed once sewn.

MAKING THE INNER POCKET

6 From the contrast blue print cut two 5in x 2½in (12.7cm x 6.4cm) rectangles. Prepare and sew five clamshells to the top edge of one of the rectangles (**Fig 3**).

8 Cut an 11½in x 5in (29.2cm x 12.7cm) rectangle from the blue tonal fabric. Following **Fig 5**, position the inner pocket on top of the lining and sew close to the bottom edge. Sew a line in the centre to make two pockets.

Fig 3

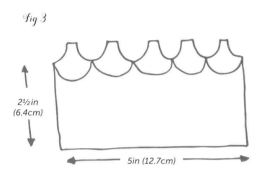

2½in
(6.4cm)

5in (12.7cm)

Fig 5

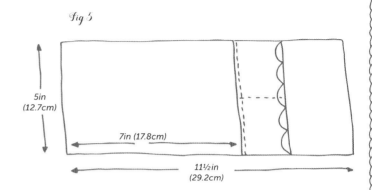

5in
(12.7cm)

7in (17.8cm)

11½in
(29.2cm)

7 Place the rectangles right sides together and sew down the long sides. Trim the excess fabric, turn to the right side, and press (**Fig 4**).

Fig 4

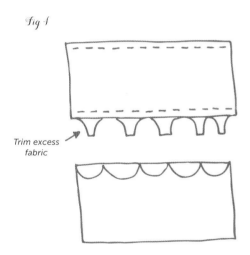

Trim excess
fabric

ADDING THE WOOL FISH NEEDLE KEEPERS

9 Using the fusible web method of appliqué, prepare the wool fish, including their fins. Refer to Basic Techniques: Fusible Web Appliqué. Using the picture as a guide for placement, position them on the lining and fuse in place. Hand sew around the edge with a blanket stitch using two strands of thread. Sew a few dashes on each tail and on the fin of the large fish, and give them a French knot for their eyes.

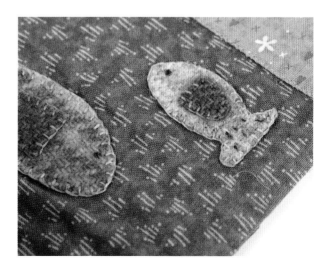

PREPARING THE NEEDLEROLL ENDS

10 Using the template provided, cut four circles from thin card and two circles from lightweight fusible wadding (batting).

11 This time adding on ¼in (6mm) seam allowance all the way around, use the template provided to cut four circles from the blue/mauve print fabric.

12 Glue a circle of wadding (batting) to a thin card circle and wait for the glue to dry. Centre the card circle on the wrong side of a fabric circle and, with the wadding (batting) facing the wrong side of the fabric, gently pull the excess fabric around the edge of the card so it is fairly taut, but not stretched. Lightly glue the seam allowance in place on the wrong side of the card. Repeat to make a second circle.

13 Glue a fabric circle around a card circle using the same method as before, but this time without wadding (batting). Repeat to make a second circle. Once the glue has dried place each one on top of a circle from Step 12, wrong sides facing. Glue together to make your two needleroll ends.

MAKING THE EMBROIDERED DOMES

14 Take one of the stitchery circles and, using a double strand of sewing thread, work a line of running stitches about ⅛in (3mm) in from the edge. Place a plastic dome on the wrong side of the fabric and gently pull on the running stitches to gather the circle tightly around the dome (**Fig 6**). Finish off the thread. Repeat with the second stitchery circle to cover the second dome.

Fig 6

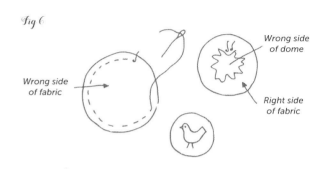

Wrong side of fabric

Wrong side of dome

Right side of fabric

15 Stitch each of the embroidered domes onto the centre of a wadding (batting) covered needleroll end. If needed, you may find it helpful to hold it in place with a small dot of craft glue before sewing.

Tip

If you are unable to find plastic domes it is easy to substitute them for self-covering buttons available from your local fabric shop. Embroider the birds, then follow the instructions on the packaging for fixing the backs in place. Then carefully cut off the shanks with a pair of pliers before attaching them to the needleroll.

ASSEMBLING THE NEEDLEROLL

16 To make the button loop cut a 1¾in x 2½in (4.4cm x 6.4cm) strip from the blue tonal fabric. Fold in half, lengthwise with right sides together and sew using a ¼in (6mm) seam. Turn to the right side and press **(Fig 7)**.

Fig 7

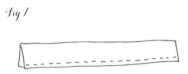

17 Cut an 11½in x 5in (29.2cm x 12.7cm) rectangle from the lightweight fusible wadding (batting). Bond to the wrong side of the lining. With right sides together place the clamshell outer on the lining and pin to hold the layers in place. Using a suitable marking pen, draw a gentle curve along the top edge of the rectangle. Fold the button loop in half and with raw edges aligned pin the button loop between the layers at the middle of the curved edge, making sure it's facing inwards **(Fig 8)**.

Fig 8

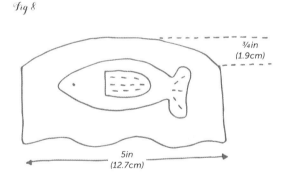

¾in (1.9cm)

5in (12.7cm)

18 Sew around the edge of the outer and lining using ¼in (6mm) seam allowance. Leave a small opening along one edge. Clip the excess fabric at the corners and turn to the right side through the opening. Press lightly, making sure that none of the lining fabric can be seen from the front and push out the corners and make sure the curve is smooth. Hand stitch the opening closed using a ladder stitch.

19 Using the template provided, cut an oval from the muddy green wool. Tack (baste) under approx. ¼in (6mm) around the edge of the stitchery and press gently **(Fig 9)**. Centre the stitchery onto the wool and, using the picture as a guide for placement, sew the wool and stitchery in place on the front of the needleroll. I used a blind hem stitch and stitched through all the layers. Remove the tacking (basting) stitches.

Fig 9

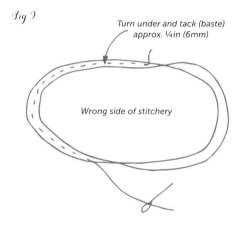

Turn under and tack (baste) approx. ¼in (6mm)

Wrong side of stitchery

20 Curl the straight end of the needleroll around the covered card circles, using the picture as a guide for how far round. Carefully stitch the covered card circle to the needleroll **(Fig 10)**. Repeat for the other end. To finish, sew the vintage mother of pearl button in place.

Fig 10

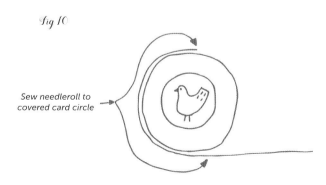

Sew needleroll to covered card circle

Ship Ahoy Snip Cover

You will need...

- ⚓ Light grey tonal fabric for the embroidery background 2¼in x 3¼in (5.7cm x 8.2cm)
- ⚓ Blue/mauve print for the lining 8in x 3in (20.3cm x 7.6cm)
- ⚓ Fusible stitchery stabilizer (optional)

- ⚓ Valdani stranded embroidery cotton (floss): #548 blackened khaki, #0578 primitive blue, #0126 old cottage grey, #H204 nostalgic rose, #154 antique gold, #JP12 seaside
- ⚓ Thin card 8in x 3in (20.3cm x 7.6cm)
- ⚓ Craft glue

Finished size

1¼in x 2¼in (3.2cm x 5.7cm) approx.

TRANSFERRING THE STITCHERY DESIGN

1. Copy the stitchery pattern (see Templates). Using a light source, such as a light box/pad or window, place the light grey tonal fabric right side up, over the stitchery pattern. Use a fabric pen to carefully trace the stitchery lines and the outer line.

WORKING THE STITCHERY

2. Use two strands of embroidery thread to stitch the design. See Techniques: Embroidery Stitches for how to work the stitches and Materials & Equipment: Threads for DMC alternatives. Stitches used are (abbreviations in brackets): backstitch (BS), satin stitch (SS), chain stitch (CHS) and French knots (FN). When stitching is completed, press gently and cut on the outer line (shown in blue on the template).

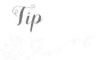

Tip

To ensure that stitchery is centred on the card, hold the stitchery up to a light source with the card shape behind. You will easily be able to see if you have it in the correct position.

CUTTING OUT

3. Using the templates provided cut the following:

   - One snip cover front from the blue/mauve fabric, adding on ¼in (6mm) seam allowance all the way around.

   - Two snip cover fronts from thin card.

   - Two snip cover backs from blue/mauve fabric, adding on ¼in (6mm) seam allowance all the way around.

   - Two snip cover backs from thin card.

MAKING THE SNIP COVER

4. Place each piece of card onto the wrong side of the appropriate fabric. Carefully put glue around the edge of the card then gently pull the ¼in (6mm) excess fabric over the edge onto the glue.

5. Once the glue has dried take both front pieces of the snip cover and, with wrong sides facing, glue the two corresponding pieces together. Hold in place whilst the glue is drying, I like to use laundry pegs to hold them together. Repeat the process for the back. You will now have a back and a front for your snip cover.

6. With two strands of Valdani floss #JP12 seaside, sew a herringbone stitch around the outer edge of the snip cover to join the front to the back (Fig 1).

Fig 1

Key for threads and stitches

 #548 Blackened khaki
Outer line (BS)

 #0578 Primitive blue
Whale's water spout (BS)
Ocean (CHS)
Lines in the ocean (BS)

 #0126 Old cottage grey
Compass outline (BS)
Compass letters (BS with FN)
Whale's eye (FN)
Needle pointing south (SS)

 #H204 Nostalgic rose
Needle pointing north (SS)
Whale's mouth (BS)

#154 Antique gold
Increments on compass (BS)

 #JP12 Seaside
Whale (BS)

Far Horizon Duffle Bag

Swing this bag over your shoulder just like a sailor heading off to sea. It's a good size for holding essential supplies such as your journal, a picnic rug and a portable sewing kit. I love designing and making practical items, and the combination of appliqué and stitchery within the lighter contrast strip make this project interesting to sew, as well as stylish to use. I chose a blue fabric to give my bag a lovely nautical feel, but you can use anything you like, just be sure to use a stronger fabric to add structure to your bag.

You will need...

- Blue yarn-dyed fabric for the bag 1½yd (1.4m)
- Light grey tonal fabric for the appliqué/stitchery background 16½in x 6½in (41.9cm x 16.5cm)
- Soft grey tonal fabric for the sea 16½in x 2½in (41.9cm x 6.4cm)
- Ten assorted 5in (12.7cm) squares for the appliqué
- Fusible stitchery stabilizer (optional)

- Valdani stranded embroidery cotton (floss): #0511 black sea, #0578 primitive blue, #078 aged wine, #154 antique gold, #P4 aged white, #548 blackened khaki
- Fusible fleece 35in x 28in (88.9cm x 71.2cm)
- Apliquick™ tools (optional)
- Appliqué paper (optional)
- Fabric glue pen (optional)

- Light box (optional)
- Fine-tipped fabric marking pen

Finished size

15½in x 18½in (39.4cm x 47cm) approx.

Use ¼in (6mm) seams unless otherwise stated.

WORKING THE APPLIQUÉ

1. Using your favourite method of appliqué, prepare the shapes, including the strip of sea (see Basic Techniques: Appliqué). If using the Apliquick™ needle-turn appliqué, as I have done, you will need to add seam allowance.

2. Photocopy or trace the stitchery design and appliqué placement template onto paper. You will need to join the design at the red dashed lines. Place on a light box and position the 16½in x 6½in (41.9cm x 16.5cm) rectangle of light grey tonal fabric on top. You can usually see through the fabric well enough to position the appliqué shapes. I like to position and either pin or glue baste in place and then stitch them all down before starting the embroidery. The black dashed lines on the appliqué templates indicate which appliqué pieces go under other appliqué shapes. Sew each shape in position using a blind hem stitch.

3. If using an iron-on stitchery stabilizer, iron it on before starting the stitching to avoid thread shadows from showing through on the front of the work. Place the shiny side of the stabilizer onto the wrong side of your fabric and follow the manufacturer's instructions to fuse it in place.

Tip

When using needle-turn appliqué, particularly for small shapes, Apliquick™ tools are extremely useful. The fabric is fused to a fusible water-soluble appliqué paper template and the tools are then used to hold the appliqué shape and turn the seam allowance over easily. This is kept in place with a stroke of fabric glue, such as a fabric glue pen which is a quick soft-drying glue designed to work with fabric and paper. The appliqué paper doesn't need to be removed – it softens as you handle it and then disintegrates when the project is washed later.

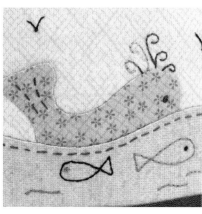

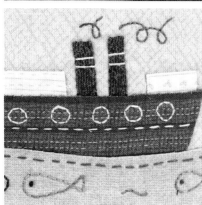
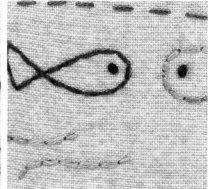

WORKING THE STITCHERY

4. Now work the stitchery. Use two strands of Valdani embroidery thread to stitch the design. See Techniques: Embroidery Stitches for how to work the stitches and Materials & Equipment: Threads for DMC alternatives. Stitches used are (abbreviations in brackets): backstitch (BS), satin stitch (SS), chain stitch (CHS), running stitch (RS) and French knots (FN).

5. Once all the appliqué and embroidery has been completed gently press your work and trim the panel to 16in (40.6cm) wide x 4¼in (10.8cm) high.

Key for threads and stitches

#0511 Black sea
Smoke (BS)
Fish eyes (FN)
Whale's eye (BS)
Markings on whale's tail (RS)

#0578 Primitive blue
Whale's water spout (BS)
Wave lines (BS)
Two fish (BS)
Dashed line under top edge of sea (RS)
Stripes on rower's shirt (RS)
Starfish (BS)

#078 Aged wine
Two fish (BS)
Flag on sailing boat (SS)
Rower's hat (SS)

#154 Antique gold
Lighthouse light (BS)
Lighthouse rays (BS)
Oar (CHS)
Two fish (BS)

#P4 Aged white
Lighthouse window (SS)
Doorknob on lighthouse (FN)
Portholes on cargo ship (BS)
Dashed line on cargo ship (RS)
Dashed lines on sailing boat (RS)
Lines on funnels (BS)
Rower's face (SS)
Mast on sailing boat (CHS)
Dashed line on sails (RS)

#548 Blackened khaki
Seagulls (BS with FN for bodies)

MAKING THE BAG

6. Using **Fig 1** for guidance, cut the following pieces from the blue yarn-dyed fabric:

- One 9¾in x 16in (24.8cm x 40.6cm) rectangle (top section of front).

- One 4in x 16in (10.2cm x 40.6cm) rectangle (bottom section of front).

- Two 2½in (6.4cm) x width of fabric (WOF) strips. Sew these together then cut into a 2½in x 70in (6.4cm x 177.8cm) strip (drawstring strap).

- One 36in x 5½in (91.4cm x 14cm) rectangle (top band).

- Three 16in x 17in (40.6cm x 43.2cm) rectangles (bag back and lining).

- Two 10½in (26.7cm) circles (bag base).

- From the remainder cut 2¼in (5.7cm) wide strips on the bias. Join them together using diagonal seams. Continue cutting and sewing the strips until you have a strip at least 35in (88.9cm) long (binding for the base).

Fig 1

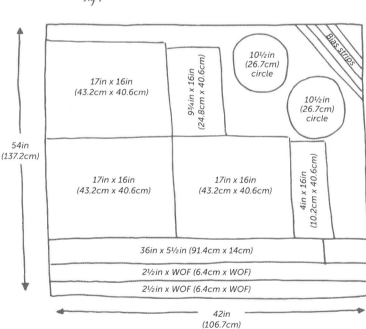

7 From the fusible fleece cut the following:

- Two 16in x 17in (40.6cm x 43.2cm) rectangles.

- One 10½in (26.7cm) circle.

8 Join the front pieces together in the following order; 16in x 9¾in (40.6cm x 24.8cm) blue yarn-dyed rectangle, 16in x 4¼in (40.6cm x 10.8cm) appliqué/stitchery panel, 16in x 4in (40.6cm x 10.2cm) blue yarn-dyed rectangle (Fig 2). Using two strands of #0578 primitive blue, add a line of large running stitches along each blue yarn-dyed piece, ¼in (6mm) away from the appliqué/stitchery panel.

Fig 2

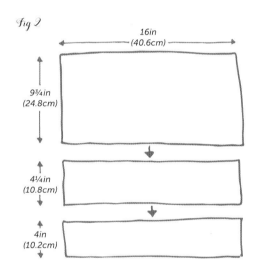

16in
(40.6cm)

9¾in
(24.8cm)

4¼in
(10.8cm)

4in
(10.2cm)

9 To make the bag outer take the two 16 x 17in (40.6cm x 43.2cm) rectangles of fusible fleece. Bond one to the wrong side of the pieced front, and the other to one of the 16in x 17in (40.6cm x 43.2cm) rectangles of blue yarn-dyed fabric. Working on a flat surface place the two pieces right sides together and sew up both 17in (43.2cm) side seams to form a tube for the outer. Press seams in one direction.

10 Take the two remaining 16 x 17in (40.6cm x 43.2cm) rectangles of blue yarn-dyed fabric and place them right sides together, as you did with the outer front, and stitch up the 17in (43.2cm) side seam to form a tube for the lining.

11 Turn the bag outer to the right side and slip this over the lining tube from Step 10. Line up the side seams. Top stitch approximately ⅛in (3mm) to one side of the seam, this will help hold the layers together.

MAKING THE TOP BAND

12 Take the 36in x 5½in (91.4cm x 14cm) rectangle for the top band and, on one of the 36in (91.4cm) sides, press in ¼in (6mm) along one edge (**Fig 3**).

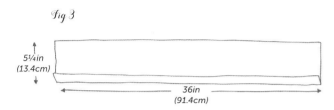

Fig 3

5¼in
(13.4cm)

36in
(91.4cm)

13 Fold the piece in half widthwise, with right sides together. Sew 2½in (6.4cm) in from the raw edge, leaving an opening as shown in **Fig 4**.

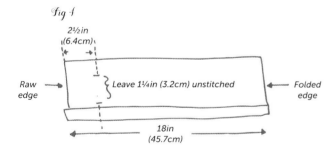

Fig 4

2½in
(6.4cm)

Raw
edge

Leave 1¼in (3.2cm) unstitched

Folded
edge

18in
(45.7cm)

14 Working on the wrong side of the fabric, fold the seam allowance back and top stitch to hold in place (**Fig 5**).

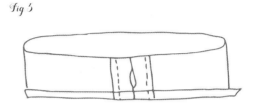

Fig 5

15 Slip the band over the main body of the bag, centring the opening at the back of the bag. When you are happy with its position pin or tack (baste) in place, then sew the band to the bag. Press the seam up away from the bag.

16 Fold the band down so the pressed ¼in (6mm) covers the sewing line and sew in place. Top stitch ¼in (6mm) in from the edge. Then add another row of top stitching ¼in (6mm) in from the top edge of the band (**Fig 6**).

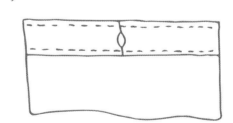

Fig 6

MAKING THE DRAWSTRING CLOSURE

17 Fold the 2½in x 70in (6.4cm x 177.8cm) strip in half and sew along the 70in (177.8cm) length (**Fig 7**). Turn to the right side and press the seam to one side.

Fig 7

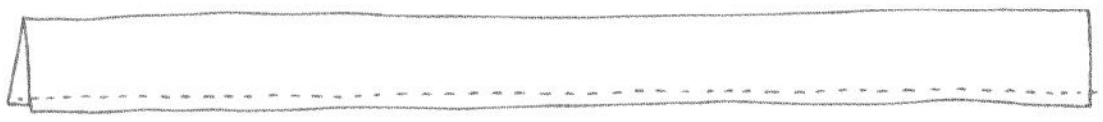

18 Sew approx. ¼in (6mm) in from each edge, along the length (**Fig 8**). Thread the drawstring through the top band.

Fig 8

SEWING THE BASE

20 Bond the fusible fleece circle to one of the blue yarn-dyed circles then place the remaining blue yarn-dyed circle on top, wrong sides together. Quilt across the fabric to hold the layers together. I quilted a cross-hatch design with the lines 1in (2.5cm) apart.

19 Lay the bag on a surface so it is flat, with the back facing you. Make sure the drawstring is fully extended within the top band and that it is not twisted. Pin the raw ends 1½in (3.8cm) either side of the centre back of the bottom of the bag. Tack (baste) the drawstring in place (**Fig 9**).

ASSEMBLING THE BAG

21 With wrong sides together, position and pin the base into the bottom of the bag and sew through all the layers.

22 Using the length of bias binding prepared in Step 6, bind the bottom edge.

Fig 9

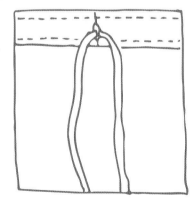

Seagull Quilt

When visiting a seaside town anywhere in the world I love to see inquisitive seagulls flying high in the sky or hunting for food around my feet. There is something about the spirit of those well-fed gulls that I wanted to capture in a quilt. The blocks are a combination of simple pieced squares and appliquéd gulls with most, but not all, facing one direction. My seagulls have been sewn with machine appliqué but they would look equally lovely finished with a hand-sewn blanket stitch. Enjoy making your very own flock of gulls to give a seaside feel to your home.

You will need...

- Light blue floral tonal fabric for the background blocks ²⁄₃yd (0.7m)
- Light grey tonal fabric for the background blocks 1yd (1m)
- Cream starfish print for the background blocks ²⁄₃yd (0.7m)
- Warm grey tonal fabric for the background blocks ¹⁄₃yd (0.4cm)
- Eighteen coordinating prints for the pieced blocks, appliqué and inner border, ¹⁄₄yd (0.25m) of each

- Light grey tonal fabric for inner border ¹⁄₂yd (0.5m)
- Soft blue tonal fabric for outer border and binding 1yd (1m)
- Two soft yellow prints for the beaks ¹⁄₈yd (0.1m) of each
- Wadding (batting) 75in (190.5cm) square
- Backing fabric 75in (190.5cm) square
- Cosmo stranded embroidery cotton (floss): #464 coral, #895 charcoal, #368 light brown, #733 mid blue

- Fusible web
- Fine-tipped fabric marking pen (removable if you prefer)

Finished size

68¹⁄₂in (174cm) square approx.

Each block is 12in (30.5cm) square

Use ¹⁄₄in (6mm) seams unless otherwise stated

CUTTING OUT

1. From the light blue floral tonal cut two 9½in (24.1cm) x width of fabric strips. Sub-cut into five 12½in x 9½in (31.8cm x 24.1cm) rectangles for the background blocks.

2. From the light grey tonal cut three 9½in (24.1cm) x width of fabric strips. Sub-cut into nine 12½in x 9½in (31.8cm x 24.1cm) rectangles for the background blocks.

3. From the cream starfish print cut two 9½in (24.1cm) x width of fabric strips. Sub-cut into five 12½in x 9½in (31.8cm x 24.1cm) rectangles for the background blocks.

4. From the warm grey tonal cut one 9½in (24.1cm) x width of fabric strip. Sub-cut into three 12½in x 9½in (31.8cm x 24.1cm) rectangles for the background blocks.

5. From the eighteen coordinating prints cut the following:

   • Eight 3½in (8.9cm) squares from each print for the blocks. This will give you 144 squares. You only need 136 of these squares for the quilt but cutting extra will give you options.

   • A total of eighty-four 1¾in x 3½in (4.4cm x 8.9cm) rectangles for the pieced border.

   • A total of four 1¾in (4.4cm) squares for the corners of the pieced border.

6. From the light grey tonal cut eight 2in (5.1cm) x width of fabric strips. Join the strips and sub-cut into two 2in x 60½in (5.1cm x 153.7cm) strips and two 2in x 63½in (5.1cm x 161.3cm) strips for the inner border.

7. From the soft blue tonal cut the following:

   • Eight 2in (5.1cm) x width of fabric strips. Join the strips and sub-cut into two 2in x 66in (5.1cm x 167.6cm) strips and two 2in x 68½in (5.1cm x 174cm) strips for the outer border.

   • Seven 2½in (6.4cm) x width of fabric strips for the binding.

MAKING THE SIXTEEN-PATCH BLOCKS

8. Take sixteen assorted 3½in (8.9cm) squares and lay them out in a design of four rows of four squares. Sew them together into rows and press the seams of row 1 and 3 in the opposite direction to rows 2 and 4. Sew the rows together to complete the block (Fig 1a–1c).

Fig 1a

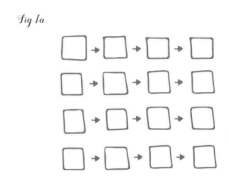

Fig 1b

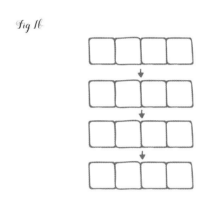

Fig 1c

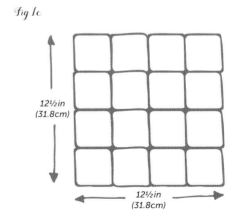

12½in (31.8cm)

12½in (31.8cm)

9. Make another two Sixteen-patch blocks in the same way, selecting the fabrics at random.

MAKING THE SEAGULL BLOCKS

10 Using your favourite method of appliqué, prepare and apply a seagull (see Templates) to each of the twenty-two 12½in x 9½in (31.8cm x 24.1cm) background rectangles. I used a fusible web method but if you prefer to use needle-turn appliqué you will need to add seam allowances to the shapes (see Basic Techniques: Appliqué). I varied the direction of the seagulls by using both sides of the template.

11 Using a suitable marking pen, transfer the templates for the seagull legs, eyes and randomly placed fish and markings on the breasts of the seagulls. Use two strands of Cosmo embroidery thread for the embroidery. See Techniques: Embroidery Stitches for how to work the stitches. Stitches used are (abbreviations in brackets): backstitch (BS), French knot (FN) and chain stitch (CHS).

Key for threads and stitches

 #464 Coral
Legs (CHS)

 #895 Charcoal
Eyes (BS with FN in centre)

 #368 Light brown
Markings on chests (randomly placed) (BS)

 #733 Mid blue
Fish in beaks (randomly placed) (BS)

SEWING THE BLOCKS TOGETHER

12 Take four assorted 3½in (8.9cm) squares and sew them together to make a row. Repeat to make a total of twenty-two rows (**Fig 2**).

Fig 2

13 Using **Fig 3** for reference, lay out the blocks. Next, place the pieced rows at the top or bottom of the seagull blocks as shown. When you are happy with the layout sew each row to a block.

Fig 3

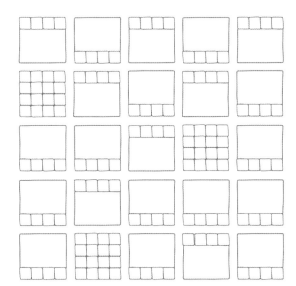

14 Sew the blocks together in rows, pressing the seams for rows 1, 3 and 5 in the opposite direction to rows 2 and 4. Now sew the rows together, pressing seams in one direction, or open if you prefer (**Fig 4**).

Fig 4

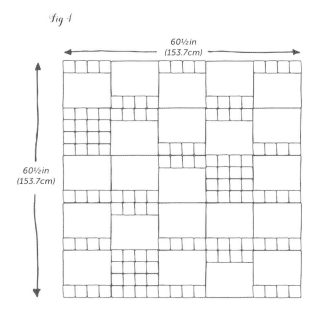

60½in
(153.7cm)

60½in
(153.7cm)

ADDING THE BORDERS

15 To add the inner border take the two 2in x 60½in (5.1cm x 153.7cm) strips and sew them to opposite sides of the quilt. Press seams outwards. Sew the two 2in x 63½in strips (5.1cm x 161.3cm) to the top and bottom of the quilt and press seams outwards.

16 The next border is pieced from the coordinating print rectangles and squares. Take twenty-one rectangles and sew them together to make a strip that measures 1¾in x 63½in (4.4cm x 161.3cm) and press the seams in one direction. Repeat to make a second pieced strip. Sew these to opposite sides of the quilt and press seams outwards. To make the top and bottom sew twenty-one rectangles together as before, but add a 1¾in (4.4cm) square at each end so the strip measures 1¾in x 66in (4.4cm x 167.6cm). Sew these to the top and bottom of the quilt and press seams outwards.

17 To add the outer border sew the 2in x 66in (5.1cm x 167.6cm) strips to opposite sides of the quilt and press the seams outwards. Finally, sew the two 2in x 68½in (5.1cm x 174cm) strips to the top and bottom of the quilt and press the seams outwards.

QUILTING AND FINISHING

18 Lay the pressed backing right side down on a surface, with the smoothed wadding (batting) on top. Lay the quilt top right side up on top, making sure there is wadding (batting) and backing showing all round, and then secure the quilt layers together (see Basic Techniques: Making a Quilt Sandwich).

19 Quilt as desired. My quilt was custom quilted with a feather and swirl design.

20 When all the quilting is finished, tidy all thread ends, square up the quilt and prepare for binding. Join the binding strips together end to end using 45-degree seams. Press the seams open. Fold the strip in half all along the length, wrong sides together and press. Use this strip to bind your quilt (see Basic Techniques: Binding).

Tip

When selecting fabrics for this quilt try to choose ones that have a fairly even tone. Avoid using fabrics that are dark or bright as they will stand out and give the project a completely different feel. One of the reasons I love this quilt is the slighty washed out soft ocean palette that makes it look calming.

All Aboard Wall Quilt and Pillow

Bring the feel of the seaside into your home with this ocean themed wall quilt and pillow. The quilt is a manageable size which means it is relatively quick to make. The techniques include simple piecing, fusible machine sewn appliqué and speedy machine quilting. I enjoyed looking through several collections to select red, blue and green fabrics that worked nicely together for these projects. Once completed, hang your quilt in pride of place at home for your family and friends to admire. The matching cushion makes an ideal gift, or why not make a set and have the boats sail along your sofa.

All Aboard Wall Quilt

You will need...

- ⚓ Fourteen assorted prints for the appliqué and border, ⅛yd (0.1m) of each
- ⚓ Four cream tonal prints for the backgrounds, ⅓yd (0.4m) of each
- ⚓ Four different cream yarn-dyed fabrics for the fish block, each 5in (12.7cm) square
- ⚓ Green print for the inner border and corner squares ¼yd (0.25m)
- ⚓ Dark cream for the seagull's beak 2in (5.1cm) square

- ⚓ Valdani stranded embroidery cotton (floss): #0511 black sea, #078 aged wine, #0578 primitive blue, #154 antique gold, #518 dusty leaves, #0178 tea, #P4 aged white, #JP12 seaside
- ⚓ Wadding (batting) 34in x 37in (86.4cm x 94cm)
- ⚓ Backing fabric 34in x 37in (86.4cm x 94cm)
- ⚓ Red stripe fabric for the binding ¼yd (0.25m)
- ⚓ Fusible web

- ⚓ One ¼in (6mm) diameter black button for the seagull's eye
- ⚓ Fine-tipped fabric marking pen
- ⚓ Light box or light pad (optional)

Finished size

28in x 31in (71.1cm x 78.7cm) approx.

Use ¼in (6mm) seams unless otherwise stated

CUTTING OUT

1 From the fourteen assorted prints cut a total of eighteen 1½in (3.8cm) squares for the blocks.

2 From the four cream tonal prints cut the backing for your blocks. You need the following:

- One 15½in (39.4cm) wide x 3½in (8.9cm) high rectangle for the Bunting block (A).

- One 5½in (14cm) square for the Compass block (B).

- One 5½in (14cm) square for the Lifebuoy block (C).

- One 10½in (26.7cm) wide x 12½in (31.8cm) high rectangle for the Sailing Boat block (D).

- One 5½in (14cm) wide x 15½in (39.4cm) high rectangle for the String of Fish block (E).

- Four different 4½in (11.4cm) squares for the Four Fish block (F).

- One 11½in (29.2cm) wide x 8½in (21.6cm) high rectangle for the Seagull block (G).

3 Cut the cream yarn-dyed fabrics into four 3½in (8.9cm) squares.

SEWING THE QUILT TOP TOGETHER

4 Select at random eight 1½in (3.8cm) squares cut from the assorted prints and sew together to make a 1½in x 8½in (3.8cm x 21.6cm) strip (**Fig 1**).

Fig 1

I have used a striped fabric for my binding which adds a lovely nautical feel. If you wish to do the same remember to buy extra binding fabric as cutting on the crossgrain (bias) uses more fabric.

5 Sew the remaining ten 1½in (3.8cm) squares cut from the assorted prints in a design five across and two down to make a 5½in x 2½in (14cm x 6.4cm) rectangle (Fig 2).

Fig 2

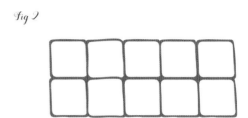

6 Sew together the four cream tonal print 4½in (11.4cm) squares for the Four Fish block to make an 8½in (21.6cm) square (**Fig 3**). Then fray approx. ¼in (6mm) around all four sides of each of the 3½in (8.9cm) cream yarn-dyed squares. Centre each frayed square onto one of the Four Fish block background squares. Using two strands of #JP12 seaside, sew a running stitch just in from the frayed edge to hold it in place (**Fig 4**).

Fig 3

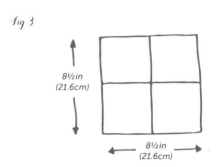

8½in (21.6cm)

8½in (21.6cm)

Fig 4

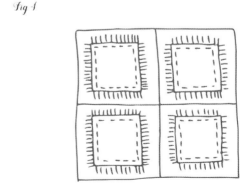

7 Referring to **Fig 5**, sew the blocks together in the following order:

Compass block (B) to the top of the 5½in x 2½in (14cm x 6.4cm) rectangle of squares and Lifebuoy block (C) to the bottom. Sailing Boat block (D) to the right of the unit followed by Bunting block (A) to the top then the String of Fish block (E) to the right. This completes the top unit.

Sew the Four Fish block (F) to the left of the 1½in x 8½in (3.8cm x 21.6cm) row of squares and the Seagull block (G) to the right. Sew this to the bottom of the top unit.

WORKING THE STITCHERY

8 Copy the stitchery design and appliqué templates for each block from the Templates section. Using a light source, such as a light box or window, centre each block right side up over the pattern and trace the stitchery lines carefully using a fine-tipped fabric pen. The string and bows that hold the bunting, and the string holding the fish are drawn freehand and both extend into the adjoining bocks. Use the picture of the quilt for guidance.

9 Use two strands of Valdani embroidery thread to stitch the design. See Techniques: Embroidery Stitches for how to work the stitches and Materials & Equipment: Threads for DMC alternatives. Stitches used are (abbreviations in brackets): backstitch (BS), chain stitch (CHS), running stitch (RS), and French knots (FN).

WORKING THE APPLIQUÉ

10 You can do the appliqué either before or after the stitchery has been completed. With this project I stitched my appliqué after. Using your favourite method of appliqué apply the motifs. I chose to use the fusible web method for my quilt and secured each motif with a machine sewn blanket stitch using matching threads (see Basic Techniques: Fusible Web Appliqué). I made the Sailing Boat block first. Each sail is assembled from three pieces. I cut and joined each sail together first and added the lines of hand stitching. The right-hand sail has a little patch which I cut from a 1in (2.5cm) square of one of my assorted prints which was slightly frayed on all four sides and attached to the sail with a running stitch using two strands of #078 aged wine. The sails were then appliquéd onto the background fabric (**Fig 6**).

Fig 6

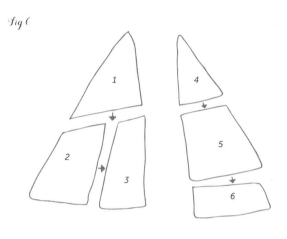

11 Using the picture as a guide for placement, continue to appliqué the blocks, adding the surface stitchery as you go.

Fig 5

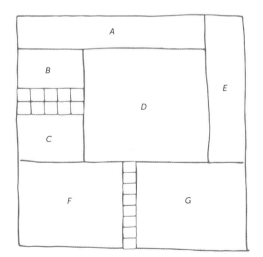

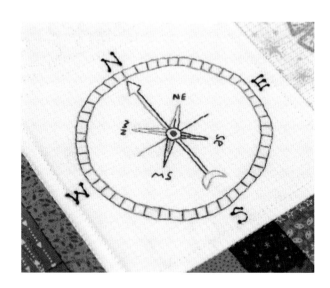

Key for threads and stitches

#0511 Black sea
Eyes for string of fish (FN)

#078 Aged wine
Dashed line on patch on sail (RS)
N, S, E and W letters on compass (BS with FN)
Bunting string and bows (CHS)
String holding the bunting flags (BS)
Ties holding flags in place (BS)

#0578 Primitive blue
Fish in seagull's mouth (BS)
Fish eye (FN)
Compass (BS)
Dashed lines on sails (RS)

#154 Antique gold
Sun (CHS)
Sun rays, outline (CHS)
Markings on sun rays (RS)
Seagull's feet (CHS)

#518 Dusty leaves
Rails on boat (CHS)

#0178 Tea
String holding little fish (BS)
Markings on seagull's chest (BS and FN)
Markings on string of fish tails (BS)
Ropes holding sails (BS)

#P4 Aged white
Dashed lines on boat hull (RS)
Rope attached to lifebuoy (place thread on drawn line and couch in place)
Markings on four fish block tails (BS)
Fish eyes on four fish block (FN)
Fish mouths on four fish block (BS)

12 From the green print cut the following:

- Two 1in x 20½in (2.5cm x 52.1cm) strips.

- Two 1in x 24½in (2.5cm x 62.2cm) strips.

- Four 4in (10.2cm) squares.

13 From the leftover fourteen assorted prints cut a total of sixty 2in x 4in (5.1cm x 10.2cm) rectangles.

14 Join one of the 1in x 20½in (2.5cm x 52.1cm) strips to the top of the centre panel and the other to the bottom, press the seams outwards. Join the 1in x 24½in (2.5cm x 62.2cm) strips to each side of the centre panel and press the seams outwards.

15 Take fourteen of the 2in x 4in (5.1cm x 10.2cm) rectangles and sew together to form a strip 4in x 21½in (10.2cm x 54.6cm). Press the seams in one direction (**Fig 7**). Sew this border to the top of your quilt and press seams outwards. Repeat to add the bottom border.

16 Take sixteen of the rectangles and sew together to form a strip 4in x 24½in (10.2cm x 62.2cm). To each end join a green 4in (10.2cm) square. Press the seams in one direction. Sew this border to one side of your quilt and press seams outwards. Repeat to add the border to the opposite side (**Fig 8**).

Fig 7

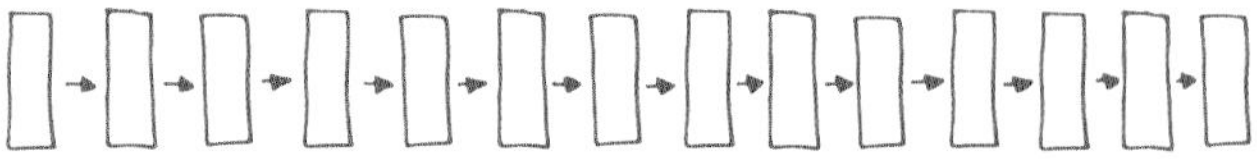

Fig 8

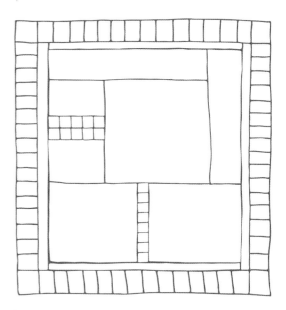

Tip

You may like to lay the rectangles around the centre panel before stitching them together; this gives you the opportunity to ensure that you are happy with the colour layout.

QUILTING AND FINISHING

17 Make a quilt sandwich of the backing fabric, wadding (batting) on top and then the front (see Basic Techniques: Making a Quilt Sandwich). Quilt as desired. My quilt was quilted using a cream thread in the centre of the quilt, and a grey and cream variegated thread in the border. Both free-motion and straight-line quilting were used. The designs are as follows:

- Feather design in the border.

- Seagull block – a wave design in the bottom half and a vermicelli pattern in the top.

- Sailing Boat block – a wave design in the bottom half, loop pattern behind the boat and echo quilting around the stitched sun.

- Four Fish, Lifebuoy and Compass blocks – straight-line quilting.

- Bunting block – loop design to fill in the background.

- String of Fish block – echo quilted around the motifs.

18 When all the quilting is finished tidy all the thread ends, square up the project and prepare for binding. Cut four 2½in (6.4cm) x width of fabric strips from the red stripe fabric. Join the strips together end to end using 45-degree seams and press seams open. Press the strip in half along the length, right sides together. Use this double-fold strip to bind the project (see Basic Techniques: Binding). Sew on the button for the seagull's eye, and add a hanging sleeve if needed.

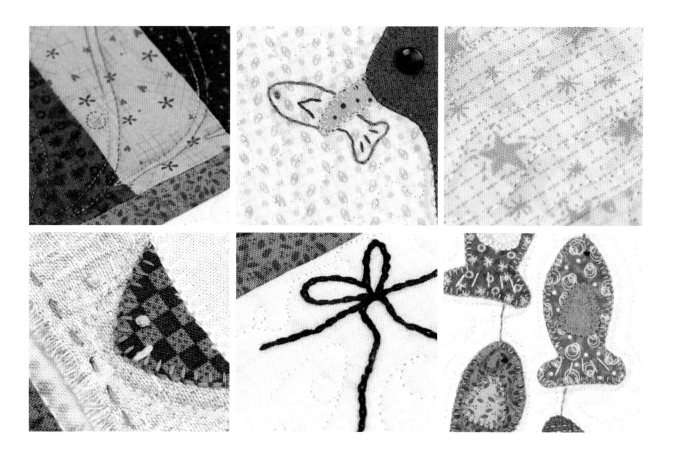

All Aboard Pillow

You will need...

- Warm cream tonal fabric for the background 12in x 14in (30.5cm x 35.6cm)
- Blue print for the boat hull 3½in x 10in (8.9cm x 25.4cm)
- Three assorted cream tonal prints for the sails and lifebuoy each 5in (12.7cm) square
- Scrap of light tan fabric for the patch on the sail
- Scraps of red print for the lifebuoy and flag
- Dark brown tonal fabric for the mast 1in x 10in (2.5cm x 25.4cm)

- Blue striped fabric for the inner border ⅛yd (0.1m)
- Red tonal fabric for the folded trim between the inner and outer border ⅛yd (0.1m)
- Thirty 2½in (6.4cm) squares from assorted dark blue prints for the outer border
- Lightweight fusible wadding (batting) 16½in x 18½in (41.9cm x 47cm)
- Dark blue print for the pillow backing 16½in x 18½in (41.9cm x 47cm)

- Valdani stranded embroidery cotton (floss): #P5 tarnished gold, #518 dusty leaves, #031 tealish blue, #0510 terracotta twist, white
- Toy filling for stuffing
- Light box or light pad (optional)
- Fine-tipped fabric marking pen

Finished size

16in x 18in (40.6cm x 45.7cm) approx.

Use ¼in (6mm) seams unless otherwise stated.

MAKING THE SAILING BOAT BLOCK

1 Take the warm cream tonal fabric. Using the picture as a guide for placement, position and apply the appliqué shapes using your favourite method of appliqué (see Basic Techniques: Appliqué). I have used the fusible web method of appliqué and stitched the blanket stitch on my sewing machine. Refer to the All Aboard Wall Quilt, Step 10, for instructions on how to appliqué the sails. The right-hand sail has a little patch which I cut from a 1in (2.5cm) square of light tan fabric which was slightly frayed on all four sides and attached to the sail with a running stitch using two strands of #0510 terracotta twist.

WORKING THE STITCHERY

2 Copy the pattern from the Templates section. Using a light source, such as a light box or window, centre the block right side up over the pattern and trace the stitchery lines carefully using a fine-tipped fabric pen.

3 Use two strands of Valdani embroidery thread to stitch the design. See Techniques: Embroidery Stitches for how to work the stitches and Materials & Equipment: Threads for DMC alternatives. Stitches used are (abbreviations in brackets): backstitch (BS), running stitch (RS), chain stitch (CHS).

4 Once the embroidery and appliqué has been completed, trim the panel to 10½in (26.7cm) wide x 12½in (31.8cm) high.

Key for threads and stitches

#P5 Tarnished gold
Sun and sun rays, outline (CHS)
Markings on sun rays (RS)

#518 Dusty leaves
Rails on boat (CHS)

#031 Tealish blue
Dashed lines on sails (RS)

White
Dashed line on boat hull (RS)
Rope attached to lifebuoy (place thread on drawn line and couch in place)
Ropes holding sails in place (BS)

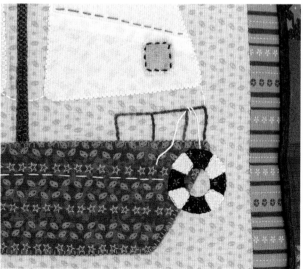

SEWING THE BORDERS

5 From the blue striped fabric cut two 1½in (3.8cm) x width of fabric strips and sub-cut them into four 1½in x 12½in (3.8cm x 31.8cm) strips. Sew two of these strips to either side of the centre panel, then the remaining two strips to the top and bottom (**Fig 1a and 1b**).

6 To create the folded trim take the red tonal fabric and cut two 1in (2.5cm) x width of fabric strips, then sub-cut into two 1in x 14½in (2.5cm x 36.8cm) strips and two 1in x 12½in (2.5cm x 31.8cm) strips.

7 Fold the red tonal strips in half lengthways, wrong sides together, and press (**Fig 2**). Align the raw edge of the 12½in (31.8cm) trims with the cut edge of the pillow on the top and bottom of the centre panel. Stitch in place with a scant ¼in (6mm) seam. Repeat for the sides of the pillow using the 14½in (36.8cm) strips.

8 For the outer border take the thirty assorted dark blue 2½in (6.4cm) squares and, working on a flat surface, arrange the squares around the centre panel. The side borders have seven squares and the top and bottom borders have eight. Once you are happy with the arrangement, sew the squares together. Attach the side borders, followed by the top and bottom (**Fig 3**).

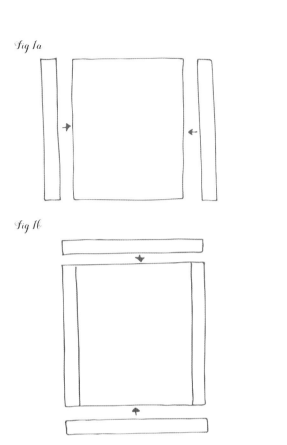

Fig 1a

Fig 1b

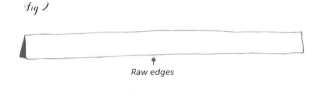

Fig 2

Raw edges

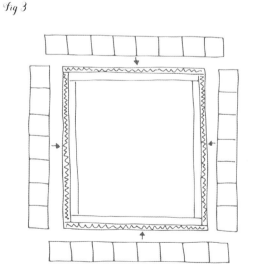

Fig 3

COMPLETING THE PILLOW

9 Bond a piece of lightweight fusible wadding (batting) to the wrong side of the pillow front.

10 Place the dark blue print backing on top of the pillow front, right sides together. Pin and stitch around the edge leaving a small opening at the bottom (**Fig 4**). Clip the excess fabric at the corners and turn the pillow through the gap so the right side is facing out. Fill the pillow with toy filling and, using thread that tones with your fabric, sew the opening closed using a ladder stitch.

Fig 4

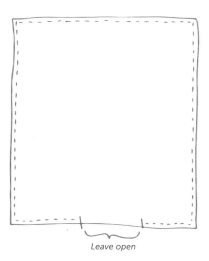

Leave open

Seafarer's Journal and Pencil Case

This stationery set is perfect to keep on your desk or to take out and about on your travels. The fabric-covered journal combines piecing, stitchery and appliqué, and is finished with one of my painted buttons to give a lovely three-dimensional feel. The journal cover is removable, so once your notebook is full you can take it off and place it on a new journal ready to record more of your hopes, dreams and wishes, or even just the shopping list. The addition of the sweet little fish toggle gives the pencil case a unique finish, and it uses an easy method to insert the zip, so do not be put off if you have never sewn one before.

Seafarer's Journal

You will need...

- A notebook to cover: mine measures 8½in x 11½in (21.6cm x 29.2cm)
- Light grey fabric for the boat background 7in x 6¾in (17.8cm x 17.1cm)
- Grey/tan fabric for the anchor background 7in x 1¾in (17.8cm x 4.4cm)
- Light blue/grey fabric for the heart background 7in x 1¾in (17.8cm x 4.4cm)
- Cream fabric for the appliqué clouds 5½in x 2½in (14cm x 6.4cm)
- Tan fabric for the appliqué boat 5in x 2in (12.7cm x 5.1cm)
- Purple fabric for the appliqué bird 2in (5.1cm) square
- White tonal print for the appliqué sails 4in x 6½in (10.2cm x 16.5cm)
- Blue/mauve print for the outer cover 23½in x 12¾in (59.7cm x 32.4cm)
- Blue striped print for the lining 23½in x 12¾in (59.7cm x 32.4cm)
- Blue fabric to fray behind the stitchery 8in x 9in (20.3cm x 22.9cm)
- Lightweight fusible fleece 23½in x 12¾in (59.7cm x 32.4cm)
- Fusible stitchery stabilizer (optional)
- Stranded embroidery cotton (floss): Valdani #P10 antique violet, #078 aged wine, #512 chimney dust, #154 antique gold, #JP12 seaside, #0126 old cottage grey, #575 crispy leaf, #514 wheat husk, #548 blackened khaki, #H204 nostalgic rose, #0511 black sea, #539 evergreens
- Fabric glue pen (optional)
- Template plastic for the sail appliqué 7in x 3in (17.8cm x 7.6cm)
- Fine-tipped fabric marking pen
- Light box or light pad (optional)
- One decorative fish button
- Lightweight fusible interfacing 6½in x 4in (16.5cm x 10.2cm)

Finished size

8½in x 11¾in (21.6cm x 29.8cm) approx.

Use ¼in (6mm) seams unless otherwise stated

PREPARING THE STITCHERY BACKGROUND

1 Sew the three background strips together, with the light grey at the top, grey/tan in the middle and the light blue/grey at the bottom (**Fig 1**).

Fig 1

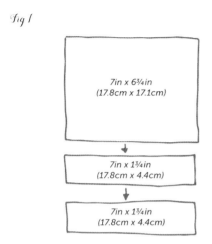

7in x 6¾in
(17.8cm x 17.1cm)

7in x 1¾in
(17.8cm x 4.4cm)

7in x 1¾in
(17.8cm x 4.4cm)

TRANSFERRING THE STITCHERY DESIGN

2 Copy the stitchery design and appliqué placement template (see Templates). You will need to join the design at the red dashed lines. Using a light source, such as a light box/pad or window, place the pieced fabric panel centrally, right side up, over the stitchery pattern. The light blue/grey fabric at the bottom will line up with the heart strip, the grey/tan fabric with the anchor strip and the light grey fabric at the top with the waves and sky. There will be excess fabric around the sides. Carefully trace the lines onto the fabric using a fine-tipped fabric pen. Fuse the stitchery stabilizer to the back of the fabric (if using).

WORKING THE APPLIQUÉ AND STITCHERY

3 Using your favourite method of appliqué, apply the boat, clouds and bird to the background fabric (see Basic Techniques: Appliqué). If using fusible web appliqué, reverse the shapes before using. I made templates for the appliqué shapes from paper, drew around the templates onto the wrong side of my chosen fabrics and cut the pieces out adding a ¼in (6mm) seam allowance. I then used needle-turn appliqué and a blind hem stitch with matching thread to sew them in place. Press the sewn shapes, first on the wrong side and then on the right side.

4 To add texture, I stitched lines of machine sewing onto the sail fabric before appliquéing. To do this trace the outer line of the two sail appliqué templates (see Templates) onto the template plastic and cut out carefully following the line. Place them on the right side of the white tonal print fabric and draw around the templates leaving a space between them to allow for shrinkage and seam allowance.

5 Following the manufacturer's instructions, bond a piece of lightweight fusible interfacing onto the wrong side of the fabric. Working with a light thread on your sewing machine, stitch across each sail. This gives texture to the sails which creates a feeling of movement (**Fig 2**).

Fig 2

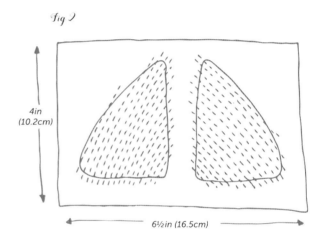

4in
(10.2cm)

6½in (16.5cm)

6 Prepare the sails for appliqué using the inner line of the sail appliqué templates. Using the same method as before, appliqué them to the background fabric.

7 Use two strands of embroidery thread to stitch the design. See Techniques: Embroidery Stitches for how to work the stitches and Materials & Equipment: Threads for DMC alternatives. Stitches used are (abbreviations in brackets): backstitch (BS), satin stitch (SS), cross stitch (CS), running stitch (RS), chain stitch (CHS) and French knots (FN).

8 When all embroidery is complete, press carefully and trim the panel to 6½in x 8¼in (16.5cm x 21cm). Around the edge, fold ¼in (6mm) to the wrong side to create a hem and tack (baste) in place. These tacking (basting) stitches will be removed later. Give the hem a good press.

Key for threads and stitches

 #P10 Antique violet
Fish below button (BS)

 #078 Aged wine
Portholes (CHS)
Star on flag (BS)
Vertical lines on bottom segment (BS)
Dots in bottom segment (FN)

 #512 Chimney dust
Triangle outline in bottom segment (BS)
Lines in bottom segment (BS)
Crosses in bottom segment (CS)
Mast (BS)

 #154 Antique gold
Sun (fill with FN)
Sun rays (RS)
Fish under bow of boat (BS)
Two little fish in anchor segment (BS)
Fin of large fish facing left on anchor segment (SS)
Bird's beak (BS)

 #JP12 Seaside
Randomly placed waves under boat (BS with FN at centre of wave)

 #0126 Old cottage grey
Seagulls (BS with FN for bodies)
Randomly placed waves under boat (BS with FN at centre of wave)
Markings on compass (BS)
N, S, E and W letters on compass (BS with FN)
Needle on compass (BS)
Ropes holding sails (BS)
Hearts in bottom segment (SS)

 #575 Crispy leaf
Crosses in row under boat (CS)
Dots in anchor segment (FN in groups of three)
Large fish facing left on anchor segment (BS)

 #514 Wheat husk
Circle lines of compass (BS)
Rope around anchor (BS)

 #548 Blackened khaki
Anchor (fill with CHS)
Lines on side of boat (BS) (note, I selected darkest colour from skein)
Outline flag (BS)

 #H204 Nostalgic rose
Bird's wing (SS)
Markings on bird's tail (RS)

#0511 Black sea
Bird and fish eyes (FN)

 #539 Evergreens
Horizontal lines dividing the segments (BS): make sure to cover the seam line

MAKING THE JOURNAL COVER

9 To cover a journal where the front cover measures approx. 8½in x 11½in (21.6cm x 29.2cm) cut a 23in x 12¼in (58.4cm x 31.1cm) rectangle from the blue/mauve print, the lightweight fusible fleece and the blue striped print.

10 Following the manufacturer's instructions, bond the fusible fleece to the wrong side of the blue/mauve rectangle.

11 Place the blue/mauve outer and blue striped print fabric right sides together and line up the edges. Stitch around the edge using ¼in (6mm) seam allowance. Leave a small opening about 3in (7.6cm) wide along the bottom edge (**Fig 3**).

Fig 3

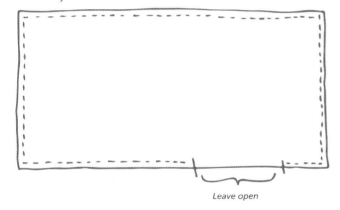

Leave open

12 Clip the excess fabric at each corner and turn to the right side through the opening. Press lightly, making sure that none of the lining fabric can be seen from the front, and push out the corners. Hand stitch the opening closed.

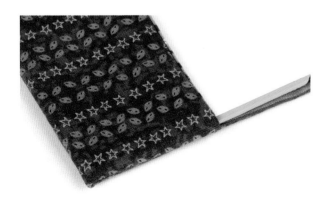

13 Lay the cover on your work surface with the lining facing you. Open your notebook and place it in the centre of the cover. Fold in the extra fabric around the cover at each end and tack (baste) in position to check the cover is a snug, but usable fit. Then neatly hand stitch in place (**Fig 4**).

Fig 4

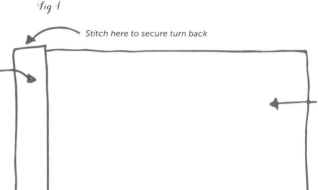

Stitch here to secure turn back

Lining

Stitch here to secure

14 Trim the blue fabric to 7in x 8¾in (17.8cm x 22.2cm) and fray approximately ¼in (6mm) of the fabric around each edge.

15 Position the frayed blue rectangle in the centre of the front cover and pin or glue in place. Centre the completed stitchery design on top of the frayed rectangle and, once you are happy with the positioning, pin or glue in position.

16 Sew the stitchery design in place using a blind hem stitch and matching thread. Using two strands of #548 blackened khaki, add a row of running stitches on the frayed blue backing just beyond the stitchery design.

17 Stitch the fish button in place and then slip the cover onto your journal.

Seafarer's Pencil Case

You will need...

- ⚓ Blue stripe fabric for the outer 9in (22.9cm) square

- ⚓ Cream fabric for the lining 9in (22.9cm) square

- ⚓ Blue/mauve fabric for the binding and tabs ⅛yd (0.1m)

- ⚓ Light grey fabric for the zip toggle 2in x 4in (5.1cm x 10.2cm)

- ⚓ Stranded embroidery cotton (floss): Valdani #JP12 seaside, #154 antique gold, #575 crispy leaf, and #H204 nostalgic rose, #512 chimney dust, #078 aged wine

- ⚓ Lightweight fusible wadding (batting) 9in (22.9cm) square

- ⚓ Fusible stitchery stabilizer (optional)

- ⚓ Two ¾in (2cm) D-rings

- ⚓ Chunky zip at least 8½in (21.6cm) long

- ⚓ Two plastic domes for the zip toggle 1¼in (3.2cm) diameter (see Suppliers)

- ⚓ Fast-tack clear-drying craft glue

Finished size

7in x 4¼in (17.8cm x 10.8cm) approx.

Use ¼in (6mm) seams unless otherwise stated

PREPARING THE OUTER

1 Take the blue stripe fabric for the outer, fusible wadding (batting) and cream lining fabric. Align the edges and prepare the layers for quilting (see Basic Techniques: Making a Quilt Sandwich).

2 Machine quilt across the fabric. I quilted a cross-hatch design with the lines approx. ½in (1.3cm) apart. Once the quilting has been completed trim the panel to 7in x 8½in (17.8cm x 21.6cm).

SEWING THE BINDING

3 From the blue/mauve fabric cut:

- Two 2¼in x 9in (5.7cm x 22.9cm) strips.
- Two 2¼in x 5in (5.7cm x 12.7cm) strips.

4 Prepare the two 2¼in x 9in (5.7cm x 22.9cm) binding strips by folding them in half lengthwise with wrong sides together and giving them a press (**Fig 1**).

5 With raw edges together and the blue stripe fabric facing you, sew a pressed binding strip to one of the 8½in (21.6cm) edges of the quilted outer. Repeat for the second 8½in (21.6cm) edge.

6 Fold the binding over to the back and hand stitch in place.

Fig 1

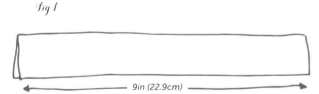

9in (22.9cm)

MAKING THE DECORATIVE TABS

7 From the blue/mauve fabric cut a 2¼in x 6in (5.7cm x 15.2cm) rectangle. Fold it in half right sides together. Sew a ¼in (6mm) seam down the length (**Fig 2**).

Fig 2

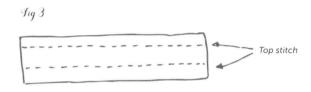

6in (15.2cm)

8 Turn the fabric through one end of the tube so the right side is facing out. Ease the seam to one side, press flat, then top stitch ¼in (6mm) in from the edge on both sides (**Fig 3**).

Fig 3

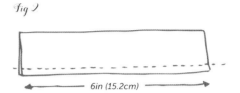

Top stitch

9 Sub-cut the strip into two 2¼in (5.7cm) long tabs.

10 Fold each tab over a D-ring. Place each one at the centre of the quilted outer with the raw edges together. Tack (baste) them in place, taking care to keep the D-ring out of the way while you sew (**Fig 4**).

Fig 4

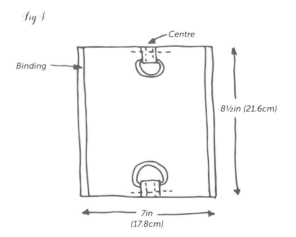

Centre

Binding

8½in (21.6cm)

7in (17.8cm)

ASSEMBLING THE PENCIL CASE

11 Position the zip under one of the bound edges. If necessary, trim the end of the zip and secure with a line of machine stitching. Then, working with a zip foot and keeping the stitching close to the edge of the binding, sew in position. For decoration, add a second row of stitching close to the first line (**Fig 5**).

Fig 5

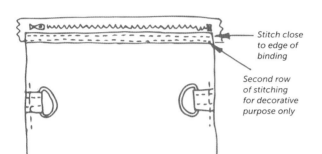

Stitch close to edge of binding

Second row of stitching for decorative purpose only

12 Repeat for the other side of the zip. You should now have a tube (**Fig 6**).

Fig 6

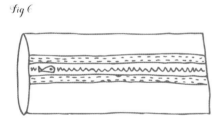

13 Slide the zip pull to the centre. Flatten the tube, making sure that the zip is centre front, then match up the sides and pin to hold the layers together (**Fig 7**).

Fig 7

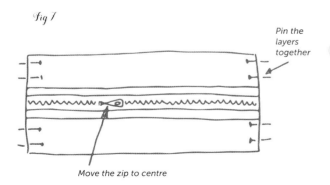

Pin the layers together

Move the zip to centre

14 Fold the 2¼in x 5in (5.7cm x 12.7cm) blue/mauve strips in half lengthwise with wrong sides together and press. With raw edges together sew one of these binding strips to each end, leaving an even amount of excess binding at the start and finish. Make sure the D-ring tabs are tucked out of the way so they do not get caught in the sewing machine (**Fig 8**).

Fig 8

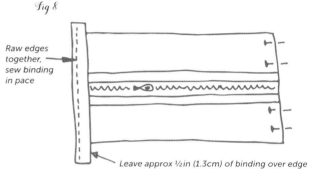

Raw edges together, sew binding in pace

Leave approx ½in (1.3cm) of binding over edge

15 Neatly finish the binding by folding in and hand sewing the excess binding at each end, then fold over the length of binding and hand sew in place (**Fig 9a and 9b**).

Fig 9a

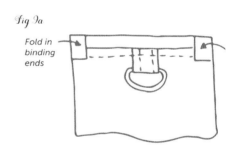

Fold in binding ends

Fig 9b

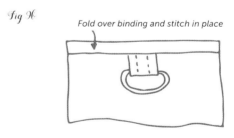

Fold over binding and stitch in place

16 Flip the tabs holding the D-rings forward and hand sew them to the binding to secure in place (**Fig 10**).

Fig 10

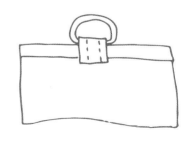

STITCHING THE ZIP TOGGLE

17 Working with the 2in x 4in (5.1cm x 10.2cm) light grey fabric, transfer the stitchery design (see Templates) twice onto the right side of the fabric. The outer line is the cutting line and includes seam allowance. Using a light source, such as a light box/pad or window, place the light grey fabric centrally, right side up, over the pattern. Carefully trace the stitchery lines onto the fabric using a fine-tipped fabric pen. If using an iron-on stitchery stabilizer, fuse it to the back of the fabric before starting the embroidery.

18 Use two strands of embroidery thread to stitch the design. See Techniques: Embroidery Stitches for how to work the stitches and Materials & Equipment: Threads for DMC alternatives. Stitches used are: backstitch (BS), satin stitch (SS), running stitch (RS) and French knots (FN).

Key for threads and stitches

#JP12 Seaside
Background dots (FN)

#154 Antique gold
Fish eye (FN)
Fish mouth (BS)

#575 Crispy leaf
Fish outline (BS)
Markings on fish tail (RS)

#H204 Nostalgic rose
Heart (SS)

ASSEMBLING THE ZIP TOGGLE

19 Once all of the embroidery is complete carefully press and cut out both of the embroidered circles following the outer line. Work a row of gathering stitches just inside the edge one of the embroidered circles. Place the plastic dome on the wrong side and gently pull the thread so the fabric fits tightly around the dome. Fasten the thread securely. Repeat with the remaining embroidered circle and second plastic dome (**Fig 11**).

Fig 11

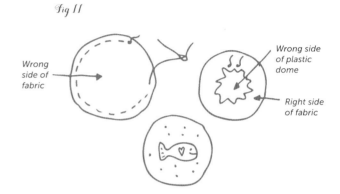

Wrong side of fabric

Wrong side of plastic dome

Right side of fabric

20 To make the twisted cord take three lengths of six ply Valdani thread #512 chimney dust about 16in (40.6cm) long. Place the threads together, anchor one end and twist the threads clockwise until the cord wants to double back on itself. Line up the ends of the threads and let the threads twist. Knot the two ends together.

21 Place the ends of the cord in between the two domes, making sure that the fish are facing the same way on each. Using the fast-tack clear-drying craft glue, join the two domes together (**Fig 12**). Once the glue has dried, sew a herringbone stitch using two strands of #078 aged wine (See Techniques: Embroidery Stitches) to cover the join where the two domes meet. Attach your fishy zip toggle to the zip and enjoy.

Fig 12

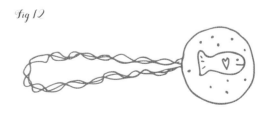

Sail Away Quilt and Pillow

I enjoyed the process of making this quilt and found choosing the colours and prints for each of the boats really satisfying. The quilt has been designed to use fabrics from your scrap stash, so when selecting your fabrics be sure to check that the pieces you choose are large enough. To give my quilt a controlled scrappy feel I have used the same print for the sails and the railings of each boat, but you could make your quilt look even scrappier by using a different print for these block components. The boats face different directions, so it looks as if they really are sailing away into the sunset.

Sail Away Quilt

You will need...

- ⚓ Fabric A (light neutral print for the background) 3⅞yd (3.6m)
- ⚓ Fabric B (assorted cream, beige, light brown and light grey fabrics) a total of ½yd (0.5m)
- ⚓ Fabric C (assorted brown and dark brown fabrics) a total of ½yd (0.5m)
- ⚓ Fabric D (assorted light blue and blue fabrics) a total of ⅝yd (0.6m)
- ⚓ Fabric E (assorted dark blue fabrics) a total of ⅜yd (0.4m)

- ⚓ Fabric F (assorted red fabrics) a total of ⅜yd (0.4m)
- ⚓ Fabric G (assorted green fabrics) a total of ⅝yd (0.6m)
- ⚓ Fabric H (assorted grey fabrics) a total of ¼yd (0.25m)
- ⚓ Wadding (batting) 66in x 77in (168cm x 196cm)
- ⚓ Backing fabric 66in x 77in (168cm x 196cm)
- ⚓ Binding fabric ⅝yd (0.6m)

Finished size

60in x 71in (152.4cm x 180.3cm) approx.

Each block is 11in (27.9cm) square

Use ¼in (6mm) seams unless otherwise stated

CUTTING OUT

1 From Fabric A (light neutral print for the background) cut the following:

FOR THE SAILBOAT BLOCKS

- Two strips 3in (7.6cm) x width of fabric. Sub-cut the strips into twenty-seven 3in (7.6cm) squares.

- Four strips 2½in (6.4cm) x width of fabric. Sub-cut the strips into fifty-four 2½in (6.4cm) squares.

- Four strips 5in (12.7cm) x width of fabric. Sub-cut the strips into fifty-four 5in x 2½in (12.7cm x 6.4cm) rectangles.

- Two strips 4½in (11.4cm) x width of fabric. Sub-cut the strips into twenty-seven 3in x 4½in (7.6cm x 11.4cm) rectangles.

- Seven strips 1in (2.5cm) x width of fabric. Sub-cut the strips into twenty-seven 1in x 9½in (2.5cm x 24.1cm) rectangles.

- Two strips 9½in (24.1cm) x width of fabric. Sub-cut the strips into fifty-four 1½in x 9½in (3.8cm x 24.1cm) rectangles.

- Two strips 11½in (29.2cm) x width of fabric. Sub-cut the strips into fifty-four 1½in x 11½in (3.8cm x 29.2cm) rectangles.

FOR THE FILLER BLOCKS

- Two strips 6in (15.2cm) x width of fabric. Sub-cut the strips into six 11½in x 6in (29.2cm x 15.2cm) rectangles.

FOR THE OUTER BORDER

- Cut seven strips 3in (7.6cm) x width of fabric. Join the strips and sub-cut into two 3in x 60½in (7.6cm x 153.7cm) strips and two 3in x 66½in (7.6cm x 168.9cm) strips.

2 From Fabric B (assorted cream, beige, light brown and light grey fabrics) cut the following:

- Nine 3in (7.6cm) squares for the sails.

- Eighteen 2½in (6.4cm) squares for the sails.

- Nine 9½in x 1in (24.1cm x 2.5cm) rectangles for the railings.

3 From Fabric C (assorted brown and dark brown fabrics) cut the following:

- Four 3in (7.6cm) squares for the sails.

- Eight 2½in (6.4cm) squares for the sails.

- Four 9½in x 1in (24.1cm x 2.5cm) rectangles for the railings.

- Nine 9½in x 2½in (24.1cm x 6.4cm) rectangles for the boats and sea.

4 From Fabric D (assorted light blue and blue fabrics) cut the following:

- Five 3in (7.6cm) squares for the sails.

- Ten 2½in (6.4cm) squares for the sails.

- Five 9½in x 1in (24.1cm x 2.5cm) rectangles for the railings.

- Nine 9½in x 2½in (24.1cm x 6.4cm) rectangles for the boats and sea.

5 From Fabric E (assorted dark blue fabrics) cut fourteen 9½in x 2½in (24.1cm x 6.4cm) rectangles for the boats and sea.

6 From Fabric F (assorted red fabrics) cut the following:

- Five 3in (7.6cm) squares for the sails.

- Ten 2½in (6.4cm) squares for the sails.

- Five 9½in x 1in (24.1cm x 2.5cm) rectangles for the railings.

- Four 9½in x 2½in (24.1cm x 6.4cm) rectangles for the boats.

7 From Fabric G (assorted green fabrics) cut the following:

- Four 3in (7.6cm) squares for the sails.

- Eight 2½in (6.4cm) squares for the sails.

- Four 9½in x 1in (24.1cm x 2.5cm) rectangles for the railings.

- Thirteen 9½in x 2½in (24.1cm x 6.4cm) rectangles for the boats and sea.

8 From Fabric H (assorted grey fabrics) cut five 9½in x 2½in (24.1cm x 6.4cm) rectangles for the boats.

9 From the binding fabric cut seven 2¼in (5.7cm) x width of fabric strips.

MAKING THE SAILBOAT BLOCKS

10 To make the first block you will need:

TWO OF THE FOLLOWING:

- 2½in (6.4cm) square Fabric D (for the sail).
- 5in x 2½in (12.7cm x 6.4cm) rectangle Fabric A.
- 2½in (6.4cm) square Fabric A.
- 1½in x 9½in (3.8cm x 24.1cm) rectangle Fabric A.
- 1½in x 11½in (3.8cm x 29.2cm) rectangle Fabric A.

ONE OF THE FOLLOWING:

- 3in (7.6cm) square Fabric A (for the sail).
- 3in (7.6cm) square Fabric D (for the sail).
- 3in x 4½in (7.6cm x 11.4cm) rectangle Fabric A.
- 9½in x 1in (24.1cm x 2.5cm) strip Fabric A.
- 9½in x 1in (24.1cm x 2.5cm) rectangle Fabric D (for the railing).
- 9½in x 2½in (24.1cm x 6.4cm) rectangle Fabric H (for the boat).
- 9½in x 2½in (24.1cm x 6.4cm) rectangle Fabric E (for the sea).

11 Draw a diagonal line on the wrong side of the 3in (7.6cm) Fabric A square. Place the square, right sides together, on the 3in (7.6cm) Fabric D square. Sew ¼in (6mm) away from, and on both sides of, the drawn line. Cut along the drawn line. Open and press to yield two half-square triangle (HST) units. Align the diagonal seam of the HST units against the 45-degree line on the quilting ruler and trim both HST units to measure 2½in (6.4cm) square (Fig 1).

Fig 1

12 Draw a diagonal line on the wrong side of a 2½in (6.4cm) Fabric D square. Place the square, right sides together, at the left-hand side of a 5in x 2½in (12.7cm x 6.4cm) Fabric A rectangle. Make sure the three sides are aligned and the diagonal line is running diagonally from the top left to bottom middle of the rectangle. Sew on drawn line. Trim ¼in (6mm) away from sewn line to remove excess fabric and then press open to reveal the corner triangle (Fig 2). Repeat to make a second unit.

Fig 2

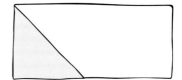

13 Sew a HST to the left-hand side of one of the units made in Step 12, making sure the triangles are facing the same way. Repeat to make a second row then sew the rows together (Fig 3).

Fig 3

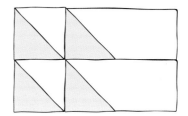

14 Sew a 3in x 4½in (7.6cm x 11.4cm) Fabric A rectangle to the left of the unit. Then sew a 9½in x 1in (24.1cm x 2.5cm) Fabric A rectangle to the bottom, followed by a 9½in x 1in (24.1cm x 2.5cm) Fabric D strip for the railing (Fig 4).

Fig 4

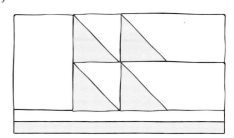

15 To make the boat take a 2½in (6.4cm) Fabric A square and draw a diagonal line on the wrong side from corner to corner. Place the square, right sides together, at one end of a 9½in x 2½in (24.1cm x 6.4cm) Fabric H rectangle. Make sure the three sides are aligned and the diagonal line is running diagonally from the top corner down towards the middle of the bottom of the boat. Sew on drawn line. Trim ¼in (6mm) away from sewn line to remove excess fabric and then press open to reveal the corner triangle. Repeat with another 2½in (6.4cm) background fabric square on the opposite side. Sew to the bottom of the unit (Fig 5).

Fig 5

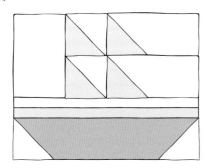

16 Next, sew the 9½in x 2½in (24.1cm x 6.4cm) Fabric E rectangle to the bottom of the unit (**Fig 6**).

Fig 6

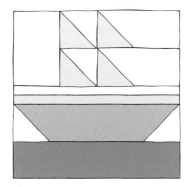

17 To add the border to the block sew two 1½in x 9½in (3.8cm x 24.1cm) Fabric A strips to opposite sides followed by a 1½in x 11½in (3.8cm x 29.2cm) Fabric A strip to the top and bottom. This completes one block (**Fig 7**).

Fig 7

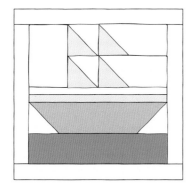

18 Repeat Steps 11 to 17 to make a total of twenty-seven blocks. Fifteen of the blocks have sails that face to the right, and twelve to the left. When you make the blocks take care at Steps 12, 13 and 14 to ensure you place the triangles in the correct position for the sails. To make the quilt you need:

- Five blocks with Fabric D sails that face to the right, Fabric D railing, Fabric H boat and Fabric E sea (**8a**).

- Five blocks with Fabric B sails that face to the right, Fabric B railing, Fabric C boat and Fabric G sea (**8b**).

- Five blocks with Fabric F sails that face to the right, Fabric F railing, Fabric E boat and Fabric D sea (**8c**).

- Four blocks with Fabric B sails that face to the left, Fabric B railing, Fabric C boat and Fabric G sea (**8d**).

- Four blocks with Fabric C sails that face to the left, Fabric C railing, Fabric G boat and Fabric D sea (**8e**).

- Four blocks with Fabric G sails that face to the left, Fabric G railing, Fabric F boat and Fabric E sea (**8f**).

Fig 8a

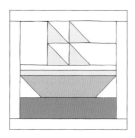

Fig 8b

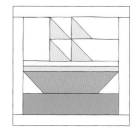

Fig 8c

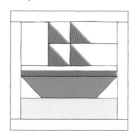

Fig 8d

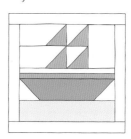

Fig 8e

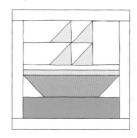

Fig 8f

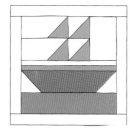

SEWING THE BLOCKS TOGETHER

19 Following the picture of the quilt lay out the blocks, alternating the direction of the sails. Place an 11½ x 6in (29.2cm x 15.2cm) Fabric A filler block at the top and bottom of columns 1, 3 and 5. Sew the blocks into columns.

20 Sew the columns together to complete the quilt centre (**Fig 9**).

Fig 9

ADDING THE BORDER

21 Sew two 3in x 66½in (7.6cm x 168.9cm) Fabric A strips to opposite sides of the quilt centre and press the seams outwards. Finally, sew a 3in x 60½in (7.6cm x 153.7cm) Fabric A strip to the top and bottom and press the seams outwards. This completes the quilt top (**Fig 10**).

Fig 10

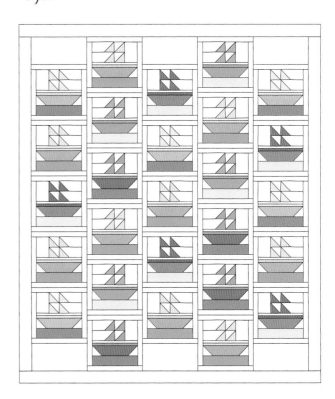

QUILTING AND FINISHING

22 Lay the pressed backing right side down, with the smoothed wadding (batting) on top. Lay the quilt top right side up on top, making sure there is wadding and backing showing all round, and then secure the quilt layers together (see Basic Techniques: Making a Quilt Sandwich).

23 Quilt as desired. I used a pale cream thread to machine quilt a fan design across the quilt.

24 When all quilting is finished, tidy all thread ends, square up the quilt and prepare for binding. Join the binding fabric strips together end to end using 45-degree seams. Press the seams open. Fold the strip in half all along the length, wrong sides together, and press. Use this strip to bind your quilt (see Basic Techniques: Binding).

Sail Away Pillow

You will need...

- ⚓ Cream tonal fabric for the background ⅛yd (0.1m)
- ⚓ Light green print for the ocean 3in x 10in (7.6cm x 25.4cm)
- ⚓ Blue tonal fabric for the boat 3in x 10in (7.6cm x 25.4cm)
- ⚓ Light blue print for the sails and railing 10in x 4½in (25.4cm x 11.4cm)
- ⚓ Twenty-two 2in (5.1cm) squares of assorted coordinating prints for the pieced border

- ⚓ Cream fabric for the pieced border ⅛yd (0.2m)
- ⚓ Dark navy print for the outer border and pillow back 20in x 16in (50.8cm x 40.6cm)
- ⚓ Fusible wadding (batting) 15½in (39.4cm) square
- ⚓ Toy filling for stuffing

Finished size

15in (38.1cm) square approx.

Use ¼in (6mm) seams unless otherwise stated

CUTTING OUT

1. From the cream tonal fabric cut the following:
   - Two 2½in (6.4cm) squares.
   - One 9½in x 1in (24.1 x 2.5cm) strip.
   - One 3in (7.6cm) square.
   - One 3in x 4½in (7.6cm x 11.4cm) rectangle.
   - Two 5in x 2½in (12.7cm x 6.4cm) rectangles.
   - Two 1½in x 9½in (3.8cm x 24.1cm) strips.
   - Two 1½in x 11½in (3.8cm x 29.2cm) strips.

2. From the light green print cut one 9½in x 2½in (24.1cm x 6.4cm) rectangle.

3. From the blue tonal fabric cut one 9½in x 2½in (24.1cm x 6.4cm) rectangle.

4. From the light blue print cut the following:
   - Two 2½in (6.4cm) squares.
   - One 3in (7.6cm) square.
   - One 9½in x 1in (24.1cm x 2.5cm) strip.

MAKING THE SAILBOAT BLOCK

5. The block is made in the same way as for the Sail Away Quilt – see Steps 11–17 in that project if required.

ADDING THE INNER BORDER

6. From the cream fabric for the border cut the following:
   - Twenty-two 2in (5.1cm) squares.
   - Six 1½in (3.8cm) squares.

7. The inner border is made up of 1in (2.5cm) half-square triangle (HST) units. To make two HST units take one print and one cream 2in (5.1cm) fabric square. On the wrong side of one of the squares draw a line diagonally from corner to corner using a suitable fabric marker (I prefer a 2B pencil). Sew ¼in (6mm) away from, and on both sides of, the drawn line. Cut along the drawn line. Open and press to yield two HST units. Align the diagonal seam of the HST unit to the 45-degree line on your quilting ruler and trim both units to measure 1½in (3.8cm) square (Fig 1a–1d).

Fig 1a

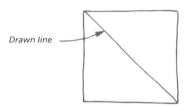

Drawn line

Fig 1b

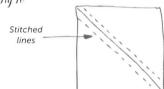

Stitched lines

Fig 1c

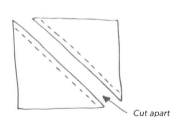

Cut apart

Fig 1d

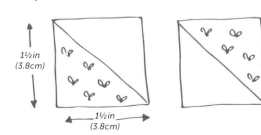

1½in (3.8cm)

1½in (3.8cm)

8 Repeat Step 7 to make a total of forty-four 1½in (3.8cm) HST units.

9 Place the block on a surface and arrange eleven HST units down both sides. Take care that the direction of the triangles is symmetrical, then sew together to make two rows (**Fig 2**). Sew the rows to the sides of the block.

10 Next, lay out the remaining HST units and 1½in (3.8cm) cream squares above and below the block. Each row should have the following in order; one square, five HSTs, one square, five HSTs, one square. Take care that the direction of the triangles is symmetrical. Sew the HSTs together to make two rows (**Fig 3**). Sew them to the top and bottom of the block.

Fig 2

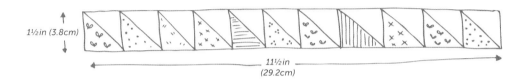

1½in (3.8cm)

11½in
(29.2cm)

Fig 3

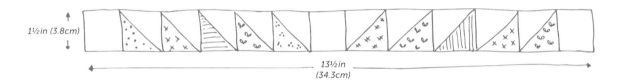

1½in (3.8cm)

13½in
(34.3cm)

ADDING THE OUTER BORDER

11 From the dark navy print cut the following:

- Two 1½in x 13½in (3.8cm x 34.3cm) strips for the side borders.

- Two 1½in x 15½in (3.8cm x 39.4cm) strips for the top and bottom borders.

- One 15½in (39.4cm) square for the back.

12 Sew the side borders to the centre panel, followed by the top and bottom borders (**Fig 4**).

COMPLETING THE PILLOW

13 Bond the square of lightweight fusible wadding (batting) to the wrong side of the completed pillow front. Quilt as desired. I free-motion quilted a swirl design across the boat, a wave design across the sea and a circle design in the outer block. The borders were quilted in the ditch.

14 Place the dark navy square on top of the pillow front, right sides together, and align the edges. Sew around the edge, leaving approximately 4in (10.2cm) open in the centre of the bottom edge (**Fig 5**).

Fig 4

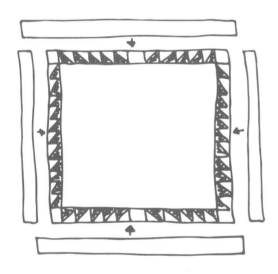

Fig 5

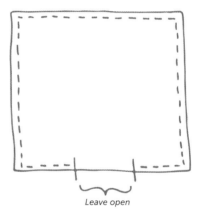

Leave open

15 Clip the excess fabric at the corners and turn the pillow through the gap so the right side is facing out. Fill the pillow with toy filling and, using thread that tones with your fabric, sew the opening closed using a ladder stitch.

Techniques

Basic Techniques

This section describes the basic techniques you will need to make and finish off the projects in this book, from transferring designs to binding a finished quilt. Beginners in particular should find it very useful.

Sewing seams

Patchwork or pieced work does require that your seams are accurate in order that your blocks will fit together nicely. Maintaining an accurate ¼in (6mm) seam allowance where stated will give the best results. For really accurate piecing sew a bare ¼in (6mm) seam, as this will allow for the thickness of thread and the tiny amount of fabric taken up when the seam is pressed.

Pressing work

Your work will look its best if you press it well. Generally, seams are pressed towards the darker fabric to avoid dark colours showing through on the right side. If joining seams are pressed in opposite directions they will nest together nicely and create the flattest join. Press (don't iron) and be very careful with steam, as this can stretch fabric, particularly edges cut on the bias.

Transferring designs

Designs can be transferred onto fabric in various ways. I use a light source, such as a light box/pad, a window or a light under a glass table. Iron your fabric so it is free of creases. Place the design right side up and then the fabric right side up on top, taping in place if necessary. Use a fine-tipped fabric marking pen or a pencil to trace the design. If the marks might show later use a temporary marker, such as an air-erasable or water-soluble one.

Using templates

The project templates are shown full size (see Templates). Please read all of the instructions with each template carefully. Once a template is the size required you can trace it onto paper or thin card, cut it out and use it as a pattern to cut the shape from fabric. Before cutting out check whether a ¼in (6mm) seam allowance is needed. If using a template for needle-turn appliqué a seam allowance will be required, but will not be needed if you are using a fusible web appliqué technique.

Templates used for fusible web appliqué will need to be reversed before use. Sometimes it is also necessary to reverse a template, so that a design will appear facing the other way. One way to reverse a template is to photocopy it and place the copy onto a light source with the template face down rather than right side up. The design is then reversed and you can trace it as normal. You could also trace the template onto tracing paper, turn the tracing paper over and trace the template again onto paper.

Patchwork

The patchwork used in the projects is described within the relevant projects but there are two patchwork units that are used more often – half-square triangles and flying geese – and these are described here.

MAKING HALF-SQUARE TRIANGLES

Some projects use half-square triangle units, sometimes in a row or to build into larger blocks. Making two half-square triangle (HST) units at once is a quick method.

 Take two squares, each different colours, and place them right sides together with the lighter square on top. Draw a diagonal line on the wrong side of the lighter square. Pin the squares together and stitch ¼in (6mm) either side of the drawn line (Fig 1a).

Fig 1a

 Cut the unit apart on the drawn line (Fig 1b) and press the seam open or towards the darker fabric (Fig 1c). Trim each unit to the correct size, ensuring the diagonal line runs across the centre of the unit.

Fig 1b

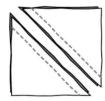

Fig 1c

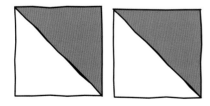

MAKING A FLYING GEESE UNIT

Some of the projects, such as the Nautical Flag Quilt, use flying geese units, to build into larger blocks. One unit will need one rectangle and two smaller squares – use the sizes given in the project instructions.

1 Draw a diagonal line on the wrong side of the two smaller squares. Place one square right sides together with a rectangle, aligning the left sides. Sew on the drawn line, from the centre top of the rectangle to the bottom left corner (Fig 2a). Trim ¼in (6mm) away from the sewn line to remove excess fabric and then press open to reveal the corner triangle.

Fig 2a

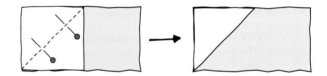

2 Repeat with the other small square on the other side of the rectangle, but this time sewing from the centre top of the rectangle to the bottom right corner (Fig 2b).

Fig 2b

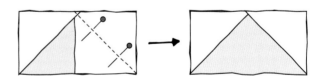

ENGLISH PAPER PIECING

This type of patchwork uses templates, usually made of paper or thin card which fabric pieces are wrapped around and tacked (basted) to. The patches are hand sewn together and the papers removed, unless you are using water-soluble liners which can be left in. Fig 3 shows the stages of a triangle being paper pieced.

1 From a master template, create enough paper templates for the project.

2. To prepare a triangle, follow **Fig 3**. Pin a paper template to a fabric shape. Cut the fabric ¼in (6mm) larger all the way around. Fold the seam allowance over the edges of the template, tacking (basting) in place through all layers. Alternatively, use a fabric glue pen. Keep the fabric firm around the paper shape and tuck in all points neatly. Repeat with all the fabric pieces.

3. Place two fabric shapes right sides together, aligning the edges, and use small whip stitches to sew together through the folded fabric but not through the paper. Place a third fabric shape right sides together with the second and sew together. Continue building the design like this. Once stitching is finished remove tacking (basting) and papers.

Fig 3

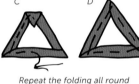 

Fold and tack (baste) or glue the fabric edges over the paper hexagon

Pre-cut paper triangle   Wrong side of fabric

Repeat the folding all round

Sew the shapes together through the fabric

Appliqué

Appliqué is the technique of applying and fixing one fabric shape on top of another. I have used two methods – needle-turn appliqué and fusible web appliqué. You may also like to use an appliqué mat.

NEEDLE-TURN APPLIQUÉ

This is a traditional method of hand appliqué where each appliqué piece has a seam turned under all round and is stitched into position on the background fabric. The appliqué shapes may be drawn freehand or templates used. See also, Using Apliquick™ Tools.

1. Mark around the template on the wrong side of your fabric and then mark another line further out all round for the seam allowance. This is usually ¼in (6mm) but it depends on the size of the appliqué piece being stitched and type of fabric being used. Smaller pieces may only need an ⅛in (3mm) allowance. Clip into the seam allowance on concave curves (the inward ones) to make it easier to turn the seam under.

2. For each appliqué piece turn the seam allowance under all round and press. Position the appliqué on the background fabric and stitch into place with tiny slipstitches. Press when finished. Some people use the needle to turn the seam under as they stitch the appliqué in place.

FUSIBLE WEB APPLIQUÉ

Fusible web has an adhesive that melts with the heat of an iron, so when the web is placed between two fabrics the heat causes the fabrics to fuse together.

1. When using templates for fusible web appliqué they need to be flipped or reversed because you will be drawing the shape on the back of the fabric – see Using Templates. If the design is symmetrical, however, you won't need to reverse it.

2. Trace around each template onto the paper side of the fusible web, leaving about ½in (1.3cm) around each shape. Cut out roughly around each shape. Iron the fusible web, paper side up, onto the wrong side of the appliqué fabric. Now cut out accurately on your drawn line.

3. When the web is cool, peel off the backing paper and then place the appliqué in position on your project, right side up. (Check the template to see which pieces need to go under other pieces, shown by dashed lines on the patterns.) Fuse into place with a medium-hot iron for about ten seconds. Allow to cool.

4. The edge of the appliqué can be further secured by stitches. I normally use blanket stitch as I like the hand-crafted look but machine satin stitch can also be used.

USING AN APPLIQUÉ MAT

Using your ironing board as a work area, lay out the appliqué mat. Remove the backing paper from each appliqué piece as required and position it on the mat. Some pieces need to go beneath other pieces and these are shown by dashed lines on templates. When positioned, iron into place on the mat. Once cool, peel the whole shape from the mat, place on the background fabric and fuse with the iron.

USING APLIQUICK™ TOOLS

These tools are a revolutionary way to prepare appliqué shapes and are used in conjunction with fusible water-soluble appliqué paper.

1 Begin by tracing the appliqué shapes onto the paper side of the appliqué paper. If you need to reverse the drawings, trace on the shiny/fusible side (**see Fig 4a**).

Fig 4a

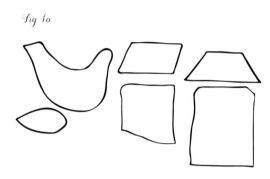

2 Cut out each shape accurately on the line. Fuse the paper shiny side down on the wrong side of the fabric. Clip all concave curves to the edge of the paper, but do not slip convex curves. Cut out about ¼in (6mm) beyond the drawn line, to allow for a seam allowance (Fig 4b).

Fig 4b

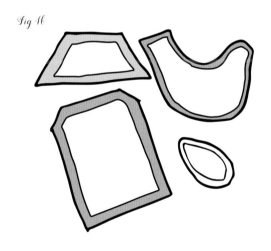

3 Place the appliqué shape face down on a flat surface. I work on a black grip mat, which prevents the shapes moving as I work. Working away from you, stroke some fabric glue onto the edge of the appliqué paper (it's ok if some glue goes on the seam allowance). I add glue in sections rather than all around the shape at once, as the glue dries into the paper fairly quickly (Fig 4c).

Fig 4c

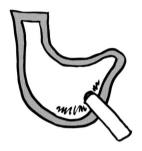

4 With the forked holding tool upright in your left hand (if right handed), rely on the weight of the tool rather than pressing down to hold the appliqué shape steady. With the bevelled-edge turning tool in your right hand and using a rolling action, slide the bevelled edge of the tool under the raw edge of the fabric and roll the seam allowance over the edge of the paper (**Fig 4d**). Press into the glue to hold the fabric seam allowance in place. Add more glue and continue working this way until the seam allowance has been turned to the wrong side around the entire shape. Press the work (**Fig 4e**). Sew the appliqué shape into position using a blind hem stitch and matching thread.

Fig 4d

Fig 4e

Adding a border

A border frames a quilt and can tie the whole design together. Borders can be plain and simple or pieced, and I have used both types in this book.

1 Calculate the length the border should be by measuring the width of the quilt through the centre. Cut the top and bottom borders to this measurement (**Fig 5a**). Sew these borders to the quilt using ¼in (6mm) seams and press.

2 Measure the quilt height through the centre, including the top and bottom borders just added (**Fig 5b**). Cut side borders to this measurement, sew them in place and press. To add a second border, repeat Steps 1 and 2.

Fig 5a

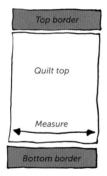

Fig 5b

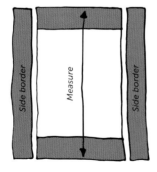

CUTTING BIAS STRIPS

Strips that are cut along the bias direction of a piece of fabric have more stretch than those cut on the straight grain and are therefore useful if you want fabric pieces to curve, for example in the Far Horizon Duffle Bag project. For a quilt or project that is bound with a straight edge you don't need bias-cut strips, but you will for any project with curves. To prepare bias-cut strips, follow Fig 6.

1 Start with a square of fabric and determine which way the bias grain is running (it will be more stretchy than the other directions). Fold the square into a triangle and crease along the bias direction.

2 Decide what width your bias strips need to be, place your fabric on the cutting board and, using a quilter's ruler, cut parallel strips across the fabric to this width.

Fig 6

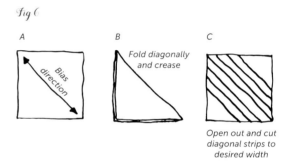

A

B   Fold diagonally and crease

C

Open out and cut diagonal strips to desired width

JOINING BIAS STRIPS

When narrow strips of fabric have to be joined, particularly bias-cut strips, they are normally joined with 45-degree seams, to make the join less noticeable. Position the two strips of fabric, right sides together, at 45-degree angles as in **Fig 7a**. Pin, sew the seam and press the seam open (**Fig 7b**).

Fig 7a

Fig 7b

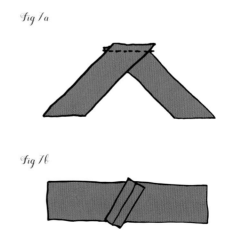

Making a quilt sandwich

A quilt sandwich is a term used to describe the three layers of a quilt – the top, the wadding (batting) and the backing. These layers need to be secured together so that a quilt will hang correctly and be free of puckers. Any hand or machine quilting you plan to do will look much better if the layers are secured well.

1. Press your backing fabric and hang out your wadding (batting) if necessary to reduce creases. Cut out your wadding and backing about 4in (10.2cm) larger than the quilt top. Prepare the top by cutting off or tying in stray thread ends, pressing it and sorting out seam allowances so they lay as flat as possible.

2. Lay the backing fabric right side down on a smooth surface and tape the corners to keep it flat. Put the wadding (batting) on top, smoothing out wrinkles. Now put the quilt top, right side up, on top.

3. Securing the three layers together can be done in various ways. Some people use pins or safety pins, some use tacking (basting), others use a spray glue. If using pins or tacking, use a grid pattern, spacing the lines about 3in–6in (7.6cm–15.2cm) apart. For fusible wadding (batting), read the manufacturer's instructions before use. Tack (baste) the outside edges of the quilt sandwich too, about ½in (1.3cm) in from the edge. The sandwich is now ready for quilting.

Quilting

Quilting not only adds texture and interest to a quilt but also secures all the layers together. I have used a combination of hand and machine quilting on the projects in this book. The hand quilting stitch is really just a running stitch and ideally the length of the stitches and the spaces in between need to be small and even. Machine quilting has a more continuous look and the stitch length is usually about 10–12 stitches per 1in (2.5cm) and may depend on the fabric and threads you are using. How much or how little quilting you do is up to you but aim for a fairly even amount over the whole quilt. When starting and finishing hand or machine quilting, the starting knot and the thread end need to be hidden in the wadding (batting).

I have described within the projects the quilting done on the projects in this book. Some areas you might consider quilting are as follows.

- Quilt in the ditch (that is, in the seams between the blocks or the units that make up the blocks).

- Echo or contour quilt around motifs, about ¼in (6mm) out from the edge of the shape.

- Background quilt in a grid or cross-hatch pattern of regularly spaced lines.

- Motif or pattern quilt within blocks or borders by selecting a specific motif, such as a heart or flower.

MARKING A QUILTING DESIGN

If you need to mark a quilting design on your top this can be done before or after you have made the quilt sandwich – most people do it before. There are many marking pens and pencils available but test them on scrap fabric first. If you are machine quilting, marking lines are more easily covered up. For hand quilting you might prefer to use a removable marker or a light pencil. Some water-erasable markers are set by the heat of an iron, so take care when pressing.

Binding

Binding a quilt creates a neat and secure edge all round. Binding may be single or double, with double-fold binding being more durable and probably best for bed quilts.

1. Measure your quilt top around all the edges and add about 10in (25.5cm) extra – this is the length of binding you need. Cut 2½in (6.4cm) wide strips (or 2¼in/5.7cm if you prefer) and join them all together to make the length needed. Fold the binding in half along the length, wrong sides together, and press.

2. Start midway along one side of the quilt and pin the binding along the edge, aligning the raw edges. Start stitching about 6in (15.2cm) away from the end of the binding and stitch through all layers using a ¼in (6mm) seam. When you reach a corner stop ¼in (6mm) away from the end (**Fig 8a**).

3. Remove the work from the machine and fold the binding up, northwards, so it is aligned straight with the edge of the quilt, creating a mitred corner (**Fig 8b**).

4. Hold the corner and fold the binding back down southwards, aligning it with the raw edge and with the folded square. Pin in position and then begin sewing again, from the top and over the fold, continuing down to the next edge (**Fig 8c**). Repeat this folding process on the other corners.

5. When you are nearing the starting point stop about 6in (15.2cm) away. Fold back the beginning and end of the binding, so they touch and mark these folds with a pin. Cut the binding ¼in (6mm) away from the pin, open out the binding and join the ends together with a ¼in (6mm) seam. Press the seam open, re-fold and press the binding, and then slipstitch in place.

6. Fold the binding over to the back of the quilt and slipstitch it in place all the way around. Fold the mitres at the corners neatly and secure with tiny slipstitches. Press the sewn binding all round to finish.

Fig 8a

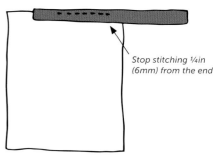

Stop stitching ¼in (6mm) from the end

Fig 8b

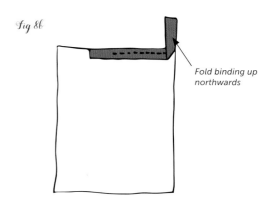

Fold binding up northwards

Fig 8c

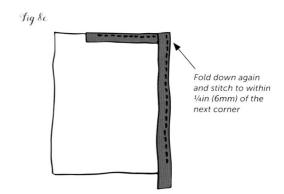

Fold down again and stitch to within ¼in (6mm) of the next corner

Labelling your quilt

When you have finished your quilt it is important to label it, even if the information you record is just your name and the date the quilt was made. When looking at antique quilts it is always interesting to piece together information about the quilt, so you can be sure that any extra information you put on your label will be of immense interest to quilters of the future. A very simple method of labelling is to write on a piece of calico with a permanent marker pen and then appliqué this to the back of your quilt. Alternatively, if you have some fabric leftover or have an extra block you can write or embroider your text onto this.

Embroidery Stitches

I have used various stitches to create the stitcheries on the projects in this book. They are all easy to work and fun to do. Follow these simple diagrams.

BLANKET STITCH

Blanket stitch can be used to edge appliqué motifs and can also be stitched in a circle for flowers. This is my version of this stitch. The conventional method often allows the thread to slip under the edges of the appliqué, allowing raw edges to be seen and this method avoids that.

Start at the edge of the appliqué shape, taking the needle through to the back of the work and come back through to the front of the shape that you are appliquéing, a small distance in from the edge where you started. Pull the thread through to form a loop. Put your needle through the loop from front to back, making sure the loop is not twisted. As you pull the thread into place lift the stitch slightly so that it sits on top of the raw edge rather than sliding underneath. Pull the thread firmly into place to avoid loose, floppy stitches. Continue on to make the next stitch.

BACKSTITCH

Backstitch is an outlining stitch that I also use to 'draw' parts of a design. It is really easy to work and can follow any parts of a design you choose.

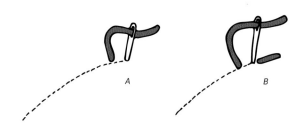

SATIN STITCH

This stitch is used to fill in areas of a design, with long stitches worked smoothly side by side.

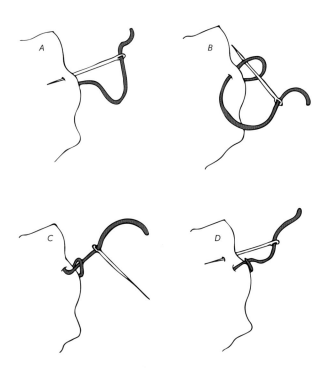

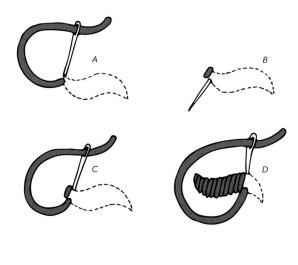

RUNNING STITCH

A running stitch is a line of evenly spaced stitches that can run in any direction or pattern you choose. Quilting stitch is a running stitch.

FRENCH KNOT

These little knots are easy to form and are useful for eyes and other details.

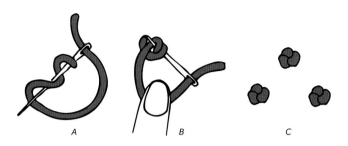

CROSS STITCH

A simple cross stitch is used in many of the stitcheries to add pattern.

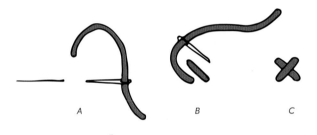

CHAIN STITCH

This stitch can be worked in straight or curved lines and also as a detached stitch. I like using it for flower and leaves.

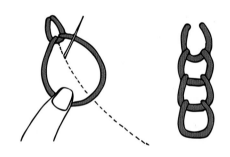

HERRINGBONE STITCH

This stitch can be used to outline areas or form patterns. It was used to stitch the Ship Ahoy Snip Cover together.

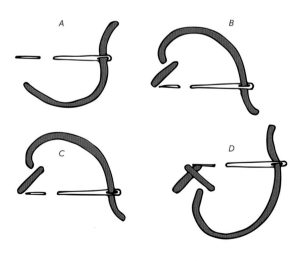

Templates

This section contains the stitchery and appliqué templates for the projects, which are all shown at full size. Templates being used for needle-turn appliqué will need to have ¼in (6mm) seam allowances added. Templates being used for fusible web appliqué will need to be reversed (flipped), unless the design is symmetrical. See Basic Techniques for Using Templates and Transferring Designs.

Nautical Flag Quilt

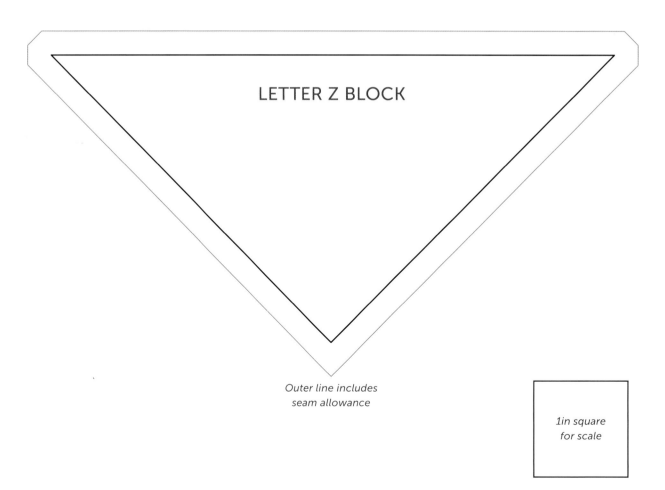

LETTER Z BLOCK

Outer line includes
seam allowance

1in square
for scale

LETTER I BLOCK

Outer line includes
seam allowance

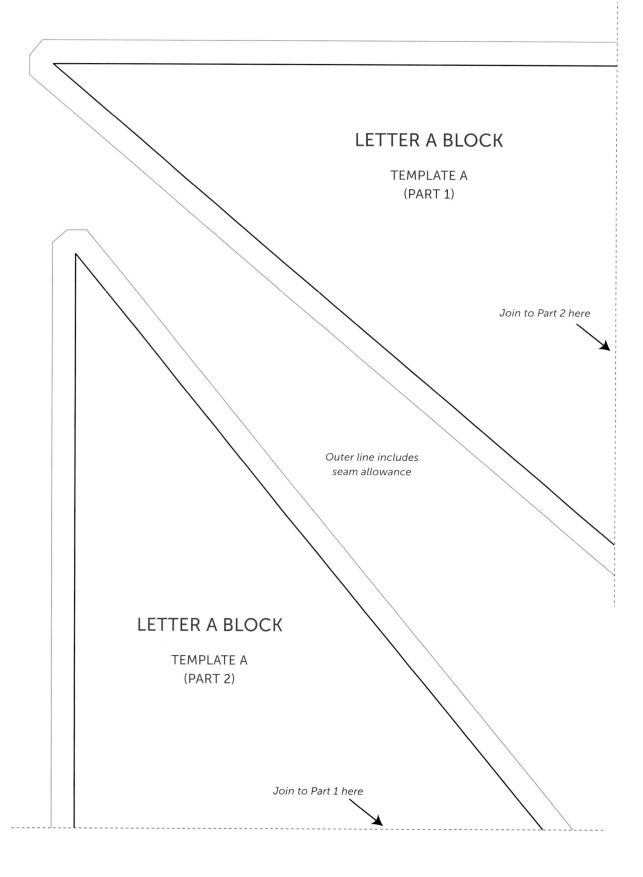

LETTER A BLOCK

TEMPLATE A
(PART 1)

Join to Part 2 here

*Outer line includes
seam allowance*

LETTER A BLOCK

TEMPLATE A
(PART 2)

Join to Part 1 here

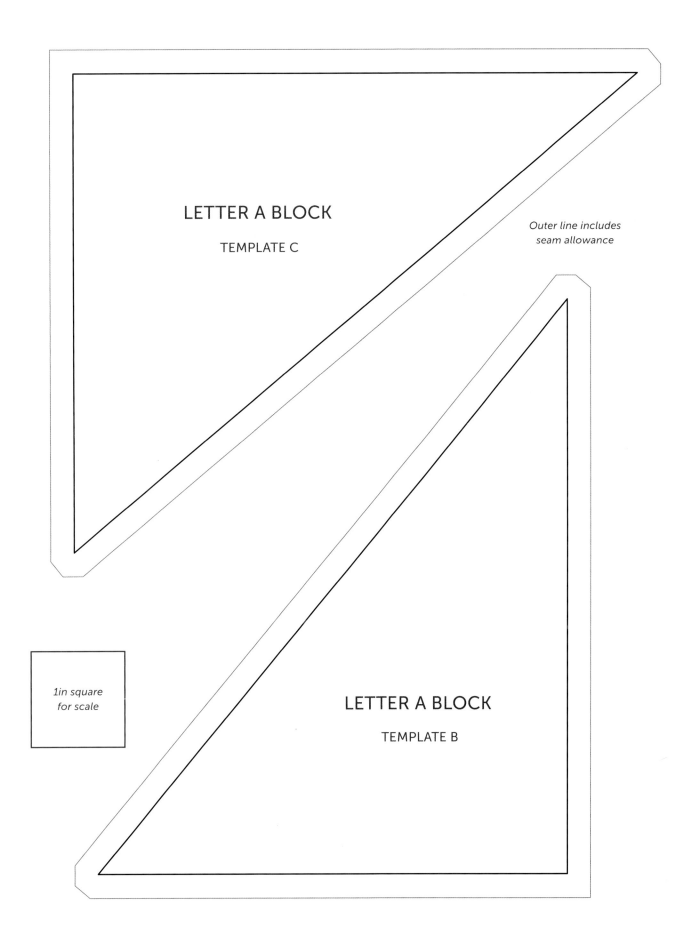

LETTER A BLOCK

TEMPLATE C

Outer line includes
seam allowance

LETTER A BLOCK

TEMPLATE B

1in square
for scale

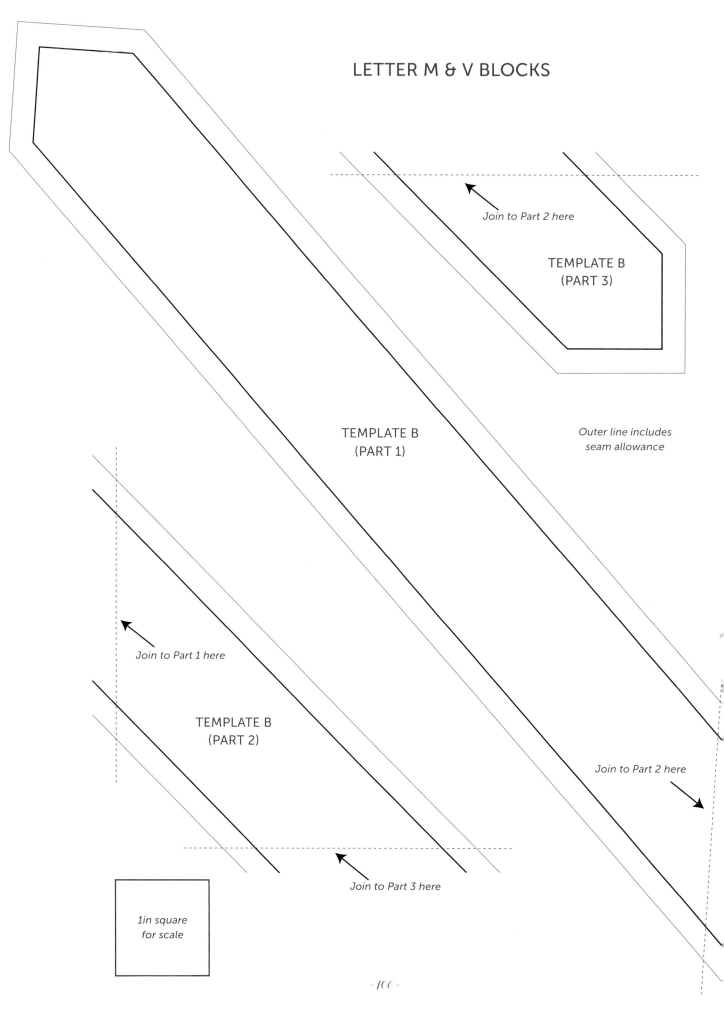

LETTER M & V BLOCKS

TEMPLATE B
(PART 3)

Join to Part 2 here

*Outer line includes
seam allowance*

TEMPLATE B
(PART 1)

Join to Part 1 here

TEMPLATE B
(PART 2)

Join to Part 2 here

Join to Part 3 here

1in square
for scale

LETTER M & V BLOCKS

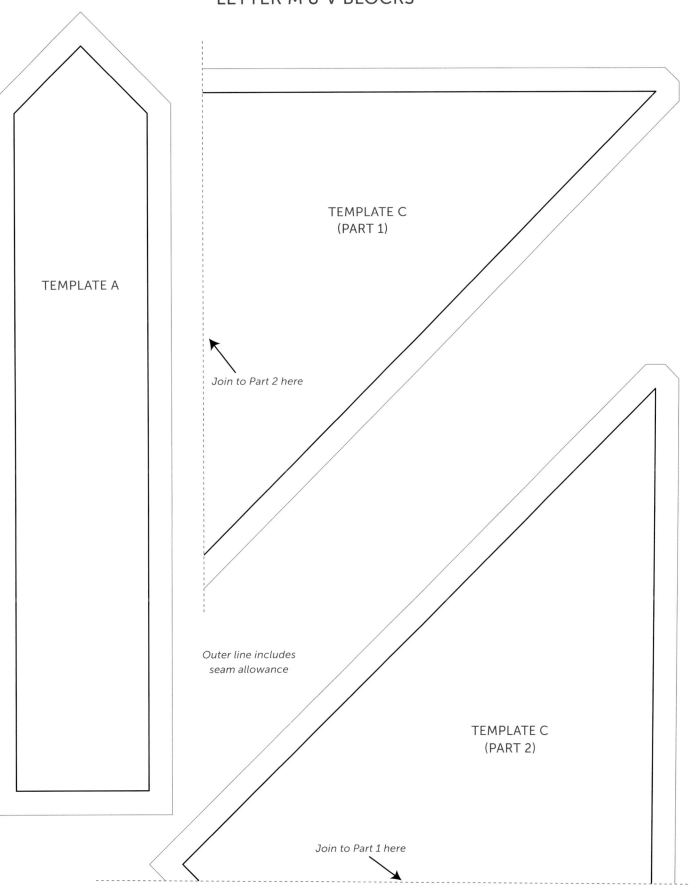

TEMPLATE A

TEMPLATE C
(PART 1)

Join to Part 2 here

*Outer line includes
seam allowance*

TEMPLATE C
(PART 2)

Join to Part 1 here

LETTER Y BLOCK

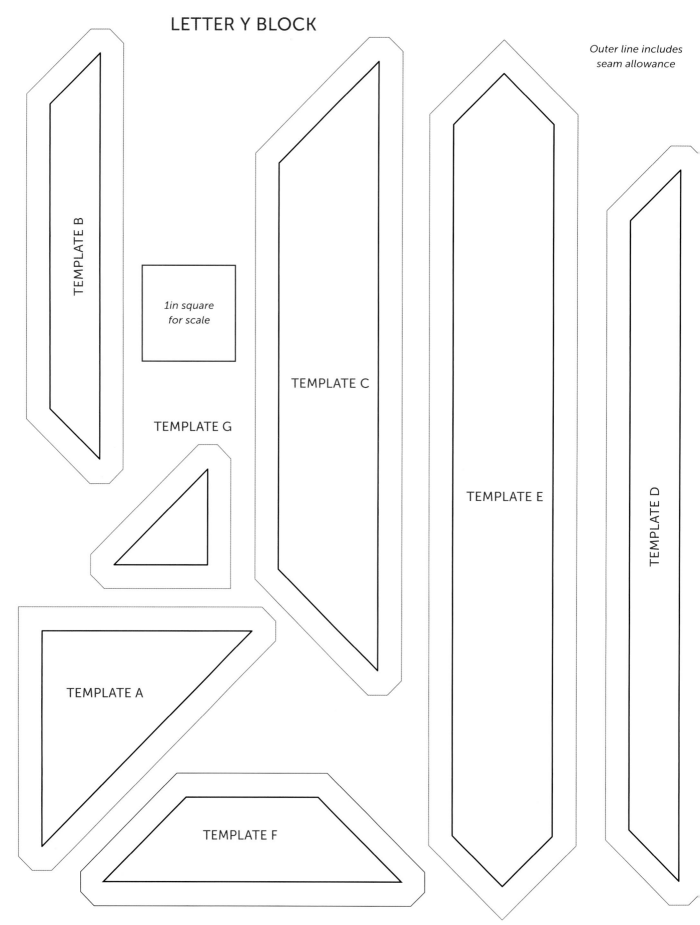

Outer line includes seam allowance

TEMPLATE B

1in square for scale

TEMPLATE G

TEMPLATE C

TEMPLATE E

TEMPLATE D

TEMPLATE A

TEMPLATE F

Storm at Sea Picture

STITCHERY DESIGN

Ship Ahoy Needleroll

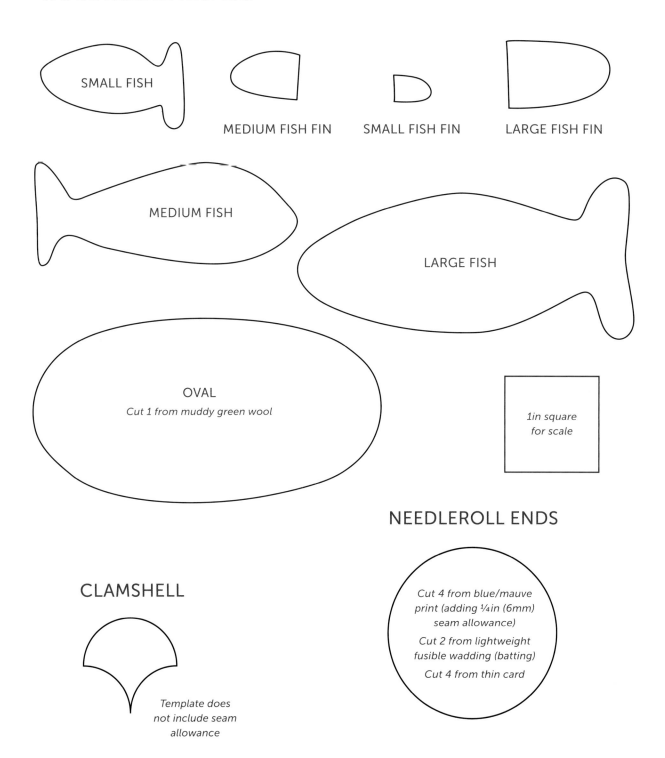

WOOL NEEDLE KEEPERS

SMALL FISH

MEDIUM FISH FIN

SMALL FISH FIN

LARGE FISH FIN

MEDIUM FISH

LARGE FISH

OVAL

Cut 1 from muddy green wool

1in square
for scale

NEEDLEROLL ENDS

*Cut 4 from blue/mauve
print (adding ¼in (6mm)
seam allowance)*

*Cut 2 from lightweight
fusible wadding (batting)*

Cut 4 from thin card

CLAMSHELL

*Template does
not include seam
allowance*

STITCHERY DESIGNS

BOAT OVAL

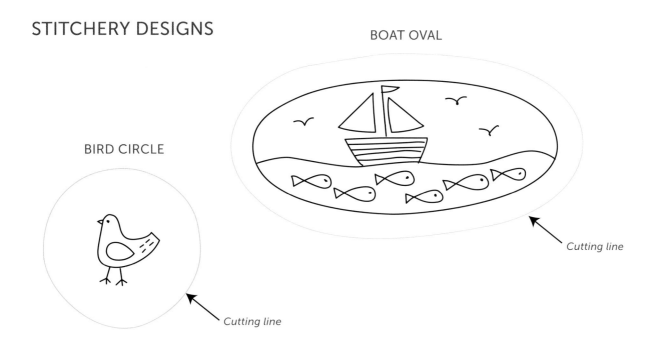

Cutting line

BIRD CIRCLE

Cutting line

Ship Ahoy Snip Cover

SNIP COVER FRONT

Cut 1 from blue/mauve fabric (adding ¼in (6mm) seam allowance)

Cut 2 from thin card

SNIP COVER BACK

Cut 2 from blue/mauve fabric (adding ¼in (6mm) seam allowance)

Cut 2 from thin card

STITCHERY DESIGN

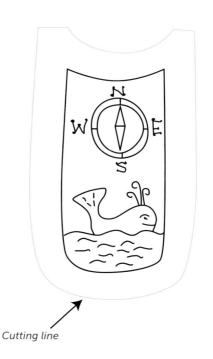

Cutting line

Far Horizon Duffle Bag

STITCHERY DESIGN AND APPLIQUÉ PLACEMENT

Red lines indicate appliqué placement

Black lines indicate stitchery lines

Green lines indicate where the surface stitchery should be

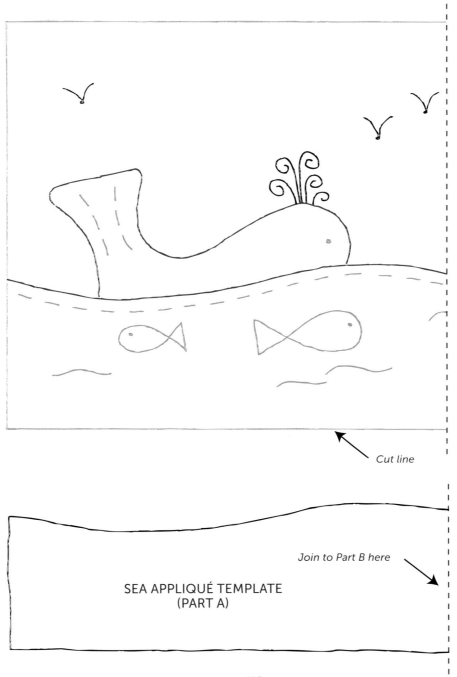

Cut line

Join to Part B here

SEA APPLIQUÉ TEMPLATE
(PART A)

1in square
for scale

Cut line

Join to Part A here

Join to Part C here

SEA APPLIQUÉ TEMPLATE
(PART B)

Far Horizon Duffle Bag

STITCHERY DESIGN AND APPLIQUÉ PLACEMENT

Red lines indicate appliqué placement
Black lines indicate stitchery lines
Green lines indicate where the surface stitchery should be

1in square
for scale

Cut line

Join to Part B here

SEA APPLIQUÉ TEMPLATE
(PART C)

APPLIQUÉ TEMPLATES

_____ *indicate an area that will be under another piece of appliqué*

If using needle-turn appliqué add ¼in seam allowance all round

If using fusible web appliqué the templates will need to be reversed

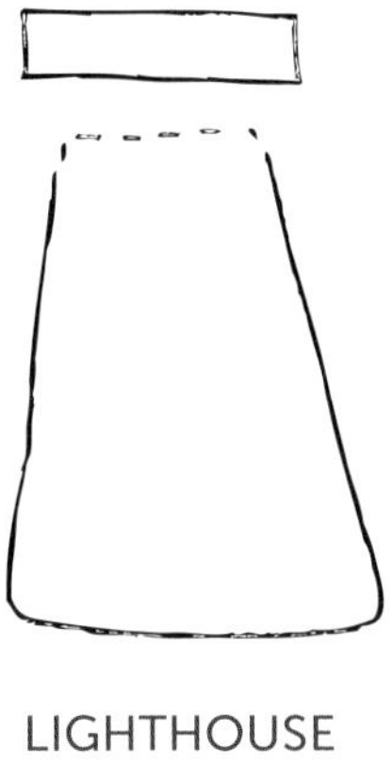

ROWING BOAT

CARGO SHIP
FUNNELS

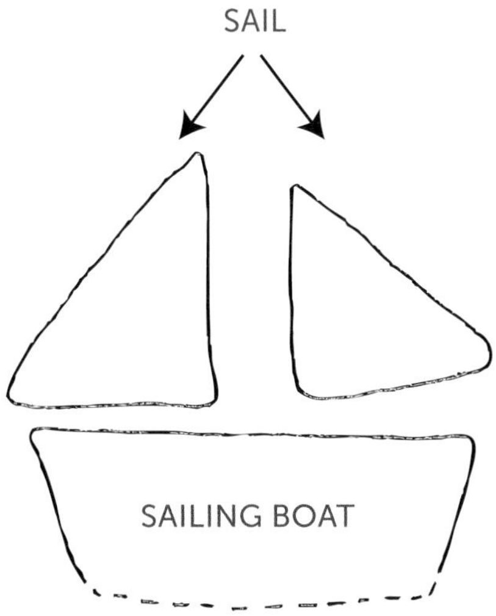

SAIL

SAILING BOAT

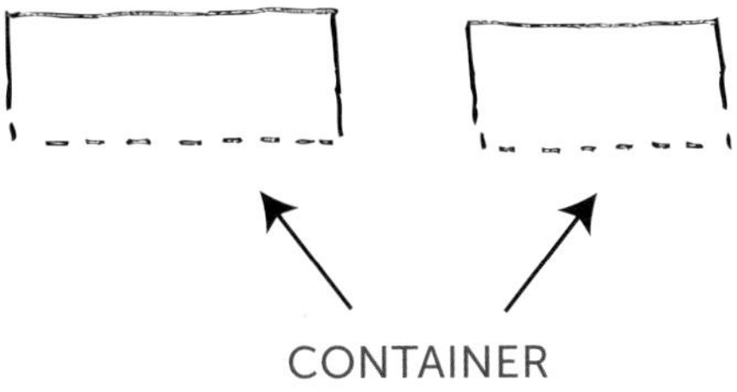

CONTAINER

CARGO SHIP

LIGHTHOUSE ROCK

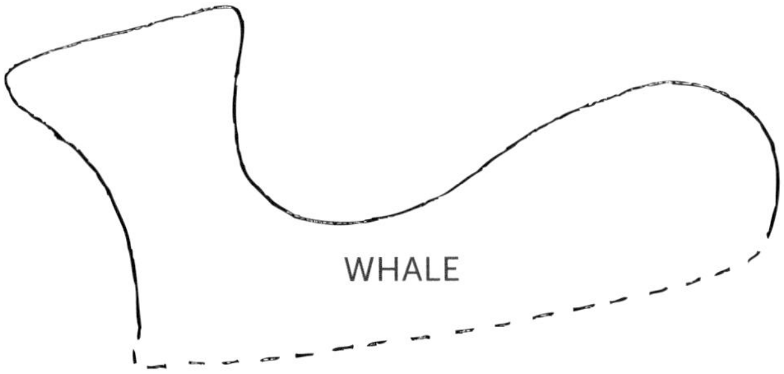

LIGHTHOUSE
DOOR

LIGHTHOUSE

WHALE

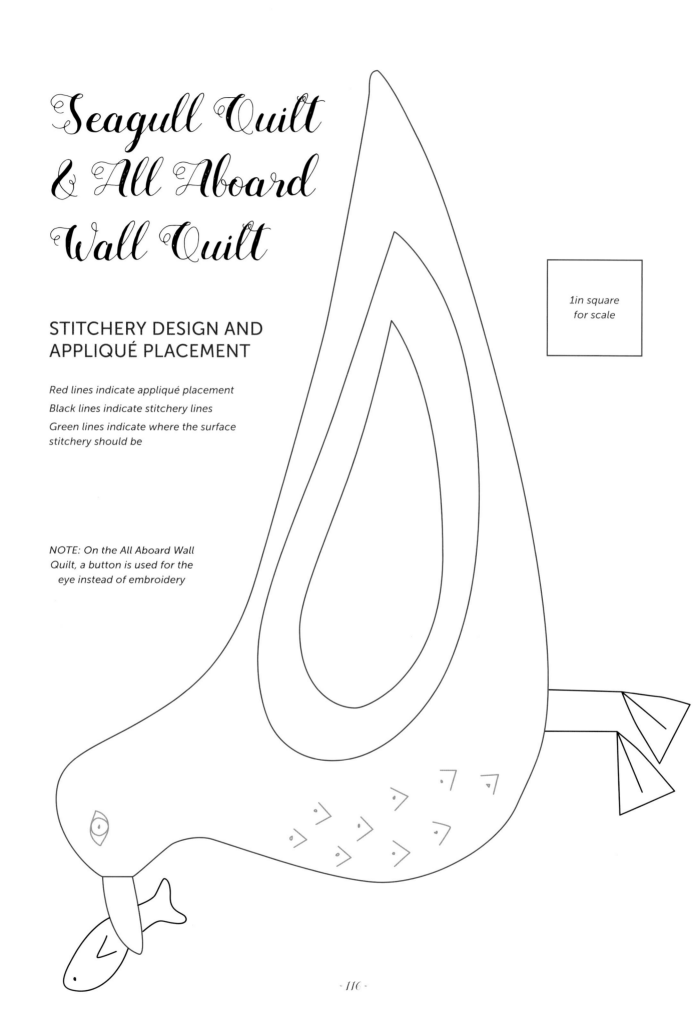

Seagull Quilt & All Aboard Wall Quilt

STITCHERY DESIGN AND APPLIQUÉ PLACEMENT

Red lines indicate appliqué placement

Black lines indicate stitchery lines

Green lines indicate where the surface stitchery should be

NOTE: On the All Aboard Wall Quilt, a button is used for the eye instead of embroidery

1in square for scale

APPLIQUÉ TEMPLATES

_____ indicate an area that will be
under another piece of appliqué

If using needle-turn appliqué add ¼in
seam allowance all round

If using fusible web appliqué the
templates will need to be reversed

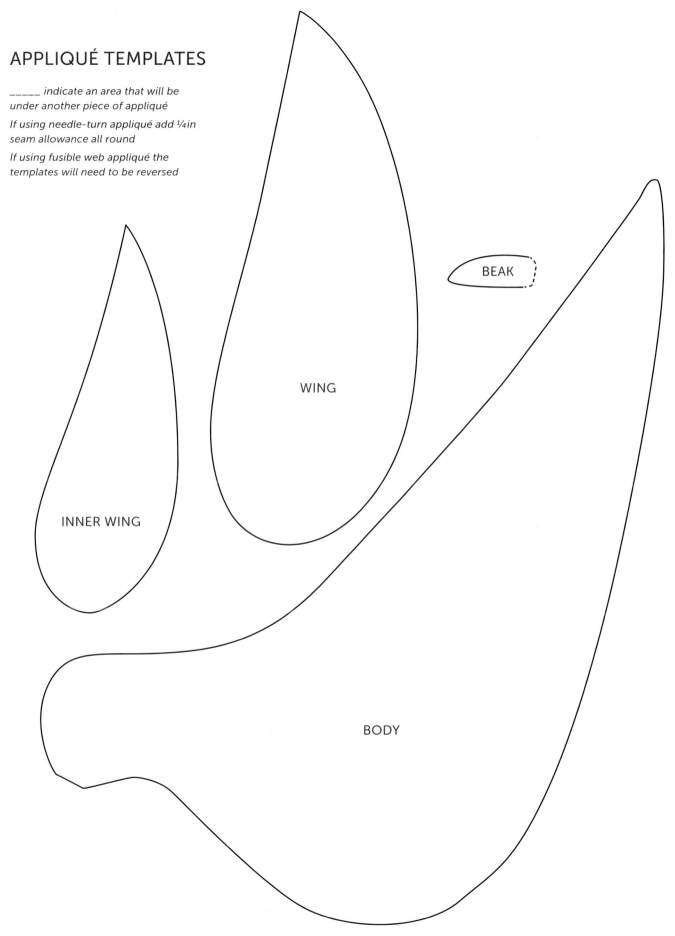

INNER WING

WING

BEAK

BODY

All Aboard Wall Quilt & All Aboard Pillow

STITCHERY DESIGN AND APPLIQUÉ PLACEMENT

Red lines indicate appliqué placement

Black lines indicate stitchery lines

Green lines indicate where the surface stitchery should be

1in square
for scale

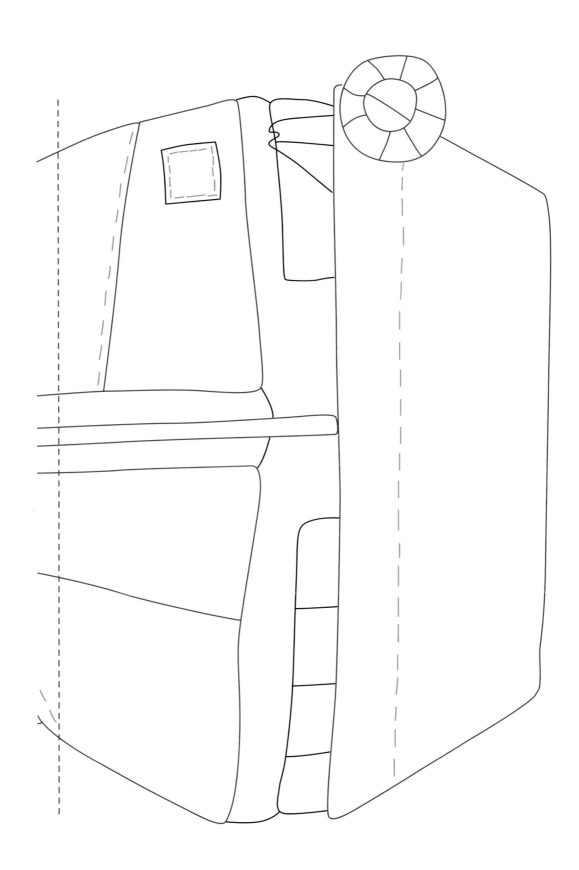

All Aboard Wall Quilt & All Aboard Pillow

1in square
for scale

STITCHERY DESIGN AND APPLIQUÉ TEMPLATES

Red lines indicate appliqué placement
Black lines indicate stitchery lines
Green lines indicate where the surface stitchery should be

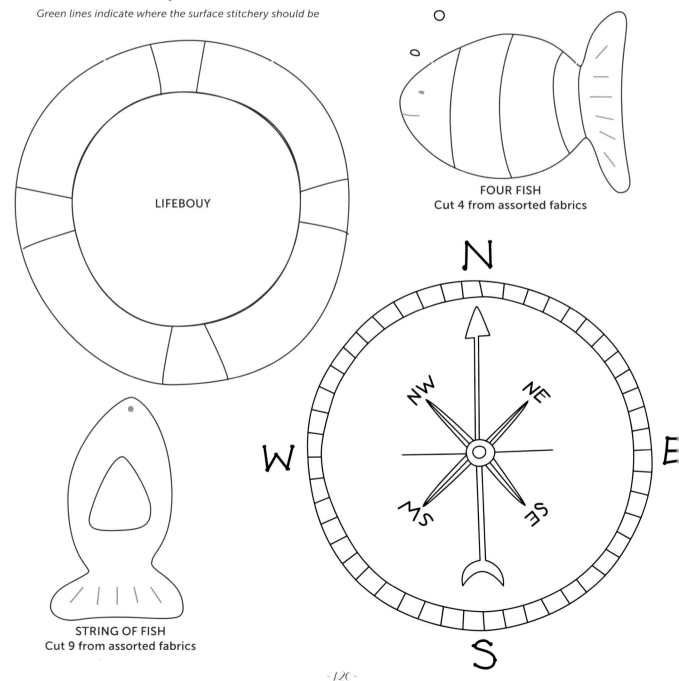

LIFEBOUY

FOUR FISH
Cut 4 from assorted fabrics

STRING OF FISH
Cut 9 from assorted fabrics

APPLIQUÉ TEMPLATES

If using needle-turn appliqué add ¼in seam allowance all round

If using fusible web appliqué the templates will need to be reversed

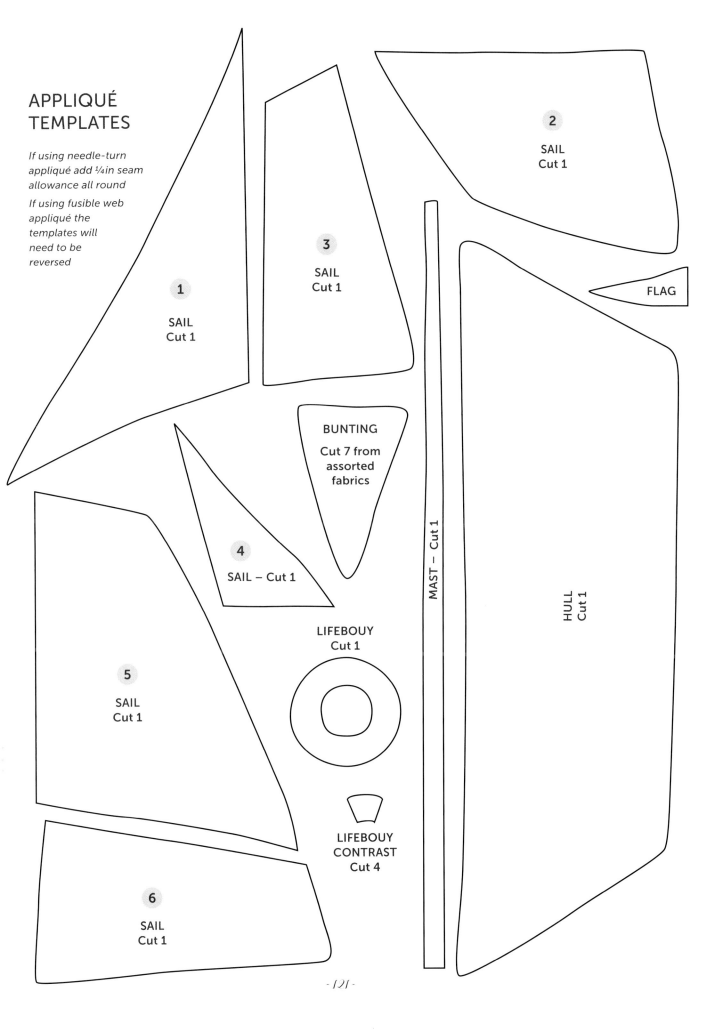

1 SAIL Cut 1

2 SAIL Cut 1

3 SAIL Cut 1

FLAG

BUNTING Cut 7 from assorted fabrics

MAST – Cut 1

HULL Cut 1

4 SAIL – Cut 1

LIFEBOUY Cut 1

5 SAIL Cut 1

LIFEBOUY CONTRAST Cut 4

6 SAIL Cut 1

Seafarer's Journal

STITCHERY DESIGN AND APPLIQUÉ PLACEMENT

Red lines indicate appliqué placement

Black lines indicate stitchery lines

Green lines indicate where the surface stitchery should be

1in square
for scale

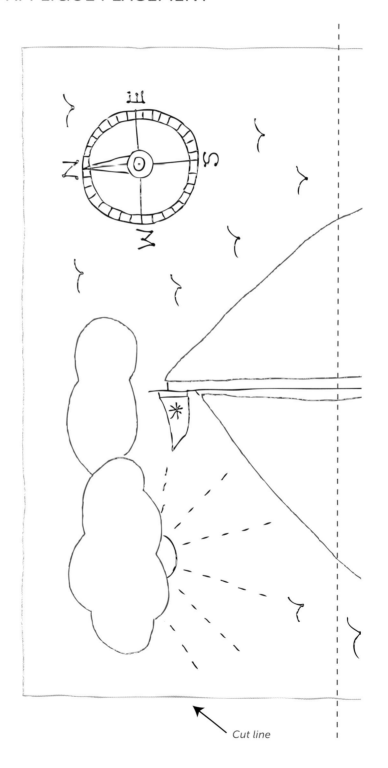

Cut line

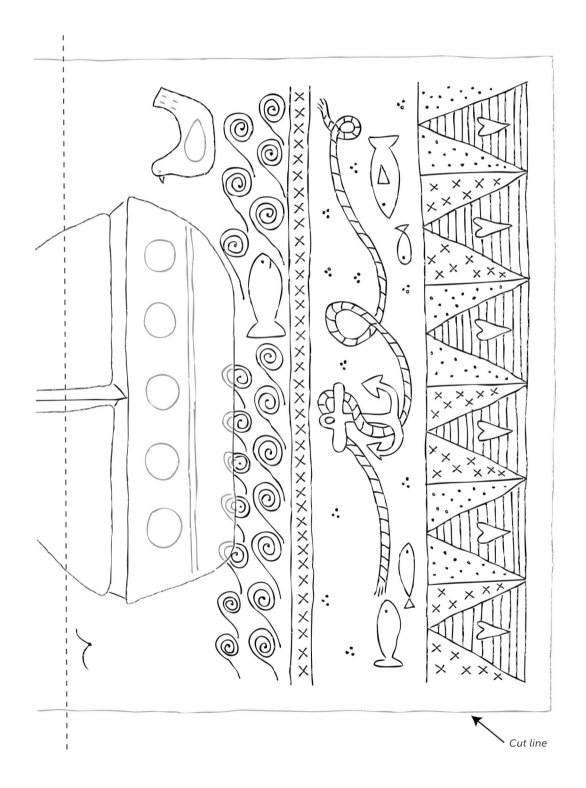

Cut line

Seafarer's Journal

APPLIQUÉ TEMPLATES

_____ *indicate an area that will be under another piece of appliqué*

If using needle-turn appliqué add ¼in seam allowance all round

If using fusible web appliqué the templates will need to be reversed

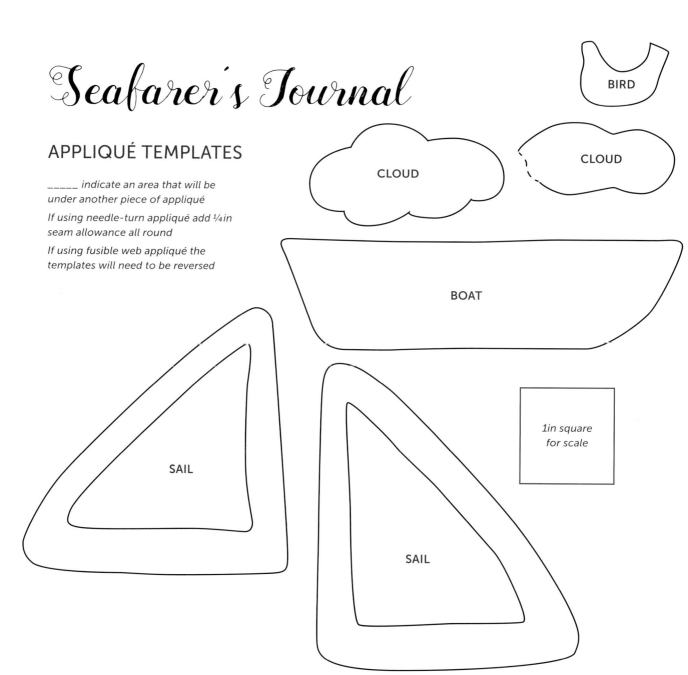

BIRD

CLOUD

CLOUD

BOAT

SAIL

SAIL

1in square for scale

Seafarer's Pencil Case

STITCHERY DESIGN

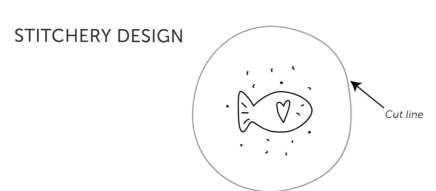

Cut line

Suppliers

Australia

LITTLE QUILT STORE

PO Box 9314
Pacific Paradise
QLD 4564
Australia
Tel: +61 (7) 5450 7497
Email: sales@littlequiltstore.com.au
www.littlequiltstore.com.au

For Lynette's books, fabrics, buttons, plastic domes, kits, Apliquick™ tools, appliqué paper, wooden frames, English paper pieces, Valdani and Cosmo stranded embroidery cotton (floss), wire quilt hangers, zips, bag parts

LYNETTE ANDERSON DESIGNS

PO Box 9314
Pacific Paradise
QLD 4564
Australia
Tel: +61 (7) 5450 7497
Email: lynette@lynetteandersondesigns.com.au
www.lynetteandersondesigns.com.au

For pattern and button wholesale enquiries and teaching information

UK & Europe

SEWANDSO

Unit 6A Delta Drive
Tewkesbury
Gloucester, GL20 8HB
UK
Tel: +44 20 3808 6645
www.sewandso.co.uk

COAST & COUNTRY CRAFTS & QUILTS

Barras Moor
Perranarworthal
Truro
Cornwall, TR3 7PE
UK
Tel: +44 1872 870478
www.coastandcountrycrafts.co.uk

CROSS PATCH

Cefn Plas
Saron, Llandysul
Carmarthenshire, SA44 5DX
UK
Tel: +44 1599 371274
Email: enquiries@cross-patch.co.uk

L'ATELIER DU PATCHWORK

L' Hotel Dieu
Villeroy, F-89 100
France

USA

VILLAGE QUILTS

17 W. Main Street
Canfield, OH 44406
USA
Tel: +1 330 533 0545
www.villagequiltscanfield.com

SEW GRACEFUL QUILTING

14094 Pleasant Ridge Road
Rogers, AR 72756
USA
Tel: +1 479 372 7403
www.sewgracefulquilting.com

About the Author

Lynette Anderson has cultivated a worldwide following unparalleled by any other designer in the quilting industry. Whether you are a lover of embellishing, stitchery, patchwork design, quilting fabric, or a bit of everything rolled into one, Lynette offers a complete package. From her rural upbringing in rural Dorset, England, Lynette has always loved the country life. She learned sewing, knitting, embroidery and painting at a very early age under the instruction of her mother, Ruth, and both her grandmothers. She stumbled into the craft of quilt making while searching for a creative outlet when her four boys were small. Her interest soon grew into a thriving career in teaching and pattern designing, and eventually to the launch of her own business, Lynette Anderson Designs, which she continued to grow after migrating with her family to Australia in 1990.

Since 1995, Lynette has published nine books, countless patterns, stitchery designs, hand-crafted wooden buttons and fifteen quilting fabric ranges, making Lynette Anderson Designs one of the most successful businesses in the quilt cottage industry. Lynette's designs are as vast as her imagination and always incorporate a touch of whimsy. Her sophisticated folk art design style is distinctive. Her unique blend of simple stitchery, appliqué and piecing in quilt design has struck a chord with embroiderers and quilters all over the world.

These days Lynette splits her time, working and designing from her home or her nearby studio and shop, which she aptly named "Little Quilt Store" nestled along the beautiful Sunshine Coast in Queensland, Australia. Lynette enjoys travelling and lecturing around the world, in the US, Japan, Canada and throughout Europe. For more information visit www.lynetteandersondesigns.com.au or follow her on Facebook, Instagram or her blog at www.lynetteandersondesigns.typepad.com.

ACKNOWLEDGMENTS

It has been a joy to design and plan the projects for this book, however without a handful of willing helpers who over the years have become my friends the projects within this book would not have been completed on time! To Donna Brabant, thank you for the wonderful piecing, machine blanket stitching, hand embroidery and for your never-ending patience sewing the bindings on. Yvonne Dann, your appliqué and embroidery skills are amazing and I am so thankful you are always such a willing helper with my projects. Thanks must also go to my friend Wendy Sheppard who helped with the maths for the Nautical Flag Quilt and Sail Away Quilt. A special thanks to my editor Elizabeth Betts without whom many important details on how to make the projects would have been forgotten. A big thank you to the team at F&W Media for their continued support in producing another lovely book.

Thank you x

Index

A SEWANDSO BOOK
© F&W Media International, Ltd 2019

SewandSo is an imprint of F&W Media International, Ltd
Pynes Hill Court, Pynes Hill, Exeter, EX2 5AZ, UK

F&W Media International, Ltd is a subsidiary of F+W Media, Inc
10151 Carver Road, Suite #200, Blue Ash, OH 45242, USA

Text and Designs © Lynette Anderson 2019
Layout and Photography © F&W Media International, Ltd 2019

First published in the UK and USA in 2019

ISBN-13: 978-1-4463-0727-4 paperback
SRN: R8726 paperback

ISBN-13: 978-1-4463-7720-8 PDF
SRN: R8674 PDF

ISBN-13: 978-1-4463-7719-2 EPUB
SRN: R8673 EPUB

Printed in China by RR Donnelley for:
F&W Media International, Ltd
Pynes Hill Court, Pynes Hill, Exeter, EX2 5AZ, UK

10 9 8 7 6 5 4 3 2 1

Content Director: Ame Verso
Acquisitions Editor: Sarah Callard
Managing Editor: Jeni Hennah
Project Editor: Elizabeth Betts
Design Manager: Anna Wade
Designers: Sarah Rowntree and Ali Stark
Illustration: Sarah Rowntree
Art Direction: Prudence Rogers
Photographer: Jason Jenkins
Production Manager: Beverley Richardson

F&W Media publishes high quality books on a wide range of subjects.
For more great book ideas visit: www.sewandso.co.uk

Layout of the digital edition of this book may vary depending on reader hardware and display settings.